Our most neglected minority asserts itself

As our techniques for prolonging life have improved, our tolerance for the natural limitations of the elderly seems to have declined. But the aging themselves are on the move. Uniting in their gray ghettos, they are beginning to organize in their own defense by taking advantage of increasingly realistic social programs catering to their needs, exercising their political muscle, and demanding a fair shake from society.

This book dramatizes the often difficult conditions older people face in this country, and it also points to hopeful signs that their raised consciousness may herald significant change.

GROWING OLD
is an original POCKET BOOK edition.

PROBLEMS OF AMERICAN SOCIETY

Focusing on the urban scene, youth, the individual and his search for a better life, the books in this series probe the most crucial dilemmas of our time.

The Negro in the City
Civil Rights and Civil Liberties
Crime and Juvenile Delinquency
Poverty and the Poor
Air and Water Pollution
The Traffic Jam
The Slums
The Draft
The City as a Community
The Consumer
Drugs
Riots
Minorities All
Governing the City
Hunger
Prisons
Racism
The Police
Political Corruption
The Family
Growing Old
**The Future*

*Forthcoming

Gordon Moss and Walter Moss

GROWING OLD

GERALD LEINWAND, General Editor

PUBLISHED BY POCKET BOOKS NEW YORK

GROWING OLD

POCKET BOOK edition published October, 1975

L

This original POCKET BOOK edition is printed from brand-new plates made from newly set, clear, easy-to-read type. POCKET BOOK editions are published by POCKET BOOKS, a division of Simon & Schuster, Inc., 630 Fifth Avenue, New York, N.Y. 10020. Trademarks registered in the United States and other countries.

1265

Standard Book Number: 671-80113-9.
 Published by POCKET BOOKS, New York, and on the same day in Canada by Simon & Schuster of Canada, Ltd., Markham, Ontario.

Front cover photograph by Nathan Farb.

Printed in the U.S.A.

ACKNOWLEDGMENTS

The authors and general editor would like to thank the writers, photographers, and publishers who permitted their works to be reprinted here. The work and cooperation of the editorial staff of WASHINGTON SQUARE PRESS is also greatly appreciated. The authors would especially like to thank their colleagues in the Southeastern Michigan Consortium on Gerontology and the Humanities, and the National Endowment for the Humanities, which has funded the consortium. If it had not been for them, this book would have never been undertaken. We also wish to acknowledge the assistance of several staff and faculty members associated with the University of Michigan-Wayne State University Institute of Gerontology, and of Mr. Charles Waller, director of the Nursing Home Ombudsman Program in Michigan.

PICTURE CREDITS

Thanks are due to the following for generously allowing us to use their photographs and illustrations in this book:

Bill Ganzel, for the photographs appearing on pages 16, 50, 55, 57, and 60, from *Depth Report #9, These Few Precious Days . . .*, School of Journalism, University of Nebraska, Lincoln.

Harper's Weekly Magazine, for the illustrations appearing on pages 21, 23, 63, 82, and 225.

Carl Fischer, for the photograph appearing on page 25.

Aging Magazine (published by the Office of Human Development, Administration on Aging, U.S. Department of Health, Education and Welfare), for the photographs appearing on pages 28, 31, 38, 53, 58, 75, 165, 180, 194, 201, and 216, and for the chart appearing on page 48.

"Good News for Later Life," New York State Legislative Document (1958), No. 8, for the photographs appearing on pages 36 and 42.

John McEnroe, for the photographs appearing on pages 40, 78, 94, 110, 158, and 232.

Joel Davis, for the photographs appearing on pages 44 and 172, from *Depth Report #9, These Few Precious Days . . .*, School of Journalism, University of Nebraska, Lincoln.

InterACTION Magazine, for the photographs appearing on pages 46, 67, 68, 76, 144, and 188.

"Brightening the Senior Years," New York State Legislative Document (1957), No. 81, for the photograph appearing on page 66.

Charities and the Commons Magazine, for the photograph appearing on page 88.

Herbold Laboratory, Inc., Hollywood, California, for the advertisement appearing on page 124.

George Lichty and Publisher's Hall Syndicate, for the GRIN AND BEAR IT cartoon appearing on page 126. Reproduced courtesy of Publisher's Hall Syndicate.

Suzanne Opton, for the photographs appearing on pages 175 and 235.

Sunrise Sales Corporation, Southfield, Michigan, for the bumper stickers used in the photographs appearing on pages 78 and 94. Bumper stickers, ©, 1974, by Sunrise Sales Corporation.

To our parents

Preface

"Crabbed age and youth cannot live together
Youth is full of pleasure, age is full of care."
William Shakespeare

The bard may not have said it all, but as you read the pages of this volume, you will discover that the cares of age today are at least as great as those to which he alluded when he wrote these well-known lines over three hundred years ago. While the pleasures of youth are often exaggerated, it is hard to overstate the cares of age. These may be summed up as loneliness, economic insecurity, anxieties over health, disappointment with children, and inability to keep creatively involved in society's affairs and in personally rewarding activities.

Ironically, the dilemmas of the aged and the aging are growing precisely because more men and women are reaching the biblical three score and ten. What one considers old may vary considerably. In some societies, the aged are those over forty. In our own, it may be said to be those over sixty-five; while in some remote places, there are men and women who are known to live regularly over the age of ninety. Yet whatever old age means chronologically, its effects are enough to make us shudder when we consider what we do with those whom society can no longer accommodate in the madcap pace it has set for itself. The aged live alone, or in old-age homes often of indifferent quality, or in the hospitals or convalescent homes where they are confined when they are chronically ill. While the aged were probably never really cared for in the bosom of the family, it is quite clear that the modern so-called nuclear family is ill-equipped to care for the aged effectively. Aggravating matters is the fact that our hierarchy of values exalts youth while denigrating age. This may be clearly seen in countless television ads, in the fear of growing old, in the constant concern for the elusive fountain of youth only temporarily found in hair dyes, cosmetic surgery, and psychiatry.

And yet there are those among us who somehow or other retain the enthusiasm of youth while tempering it with the wisdom of experience. Thus, a woman aged eighty-nine advised, "Don't say anything to me about age. Find something you did when you were young—whatever you loved, sewing or cooking or painting—and concentrate on it." Having the leisure to develop a skill neglected in younger years is one of the real joys of growing older. Yet the overwhelming majority of the aged are unable, emotionally as well as physically, to do this.

As with other volumes in this series, this is but an introductory study of a complex problem. While aging is not a problem of America alone, in many ways—because America is the womb of youthful expectations—it is here that the problems of the aged may be said to be most sharply etched. Moreover, they are by no means the problems of old people alone. They are, in fact, one of the many problems of the young; for how the young prepare for the inevitable passage of time in large measure determines what their own lives will be like in years to come.

While it may be unpleasant to contemplate aging, it may well be said that it is better than the only other possible alternative. Under the circumstances, we hope that this book will be read by young and old alike, by the former so that they may find comfort in growing old and by the latter so that they may find hope through awareness that they are not alone and courage through realizing that there are, after all, those who care.

G. L.

Contents

Part One

The Problem and the Challenge

BILL GANZEL

Counting every penny becomes an unfortunate necessity for many of the elderly.

AN OLD WOMAN turned quickly away from the dismal scene outside her Florida hotel room window. Listlessly, she mixed her own breakfast: a cup of Sanka and a small glass of Tang. After finishing her breakfast, she looked at her wardrobe. It contained a few unwanted dresses given to her by a relative, and one she had bought herself seven years ago. After choosing one, she made her bed and dusted her dresser, two small tables, and their lamps. She then turned on a small fan in anticipation of a hot muggy day, wound her clock, straightened her small pile of old books, blew dust from the artificial flowers in a cheap vase, and sat down in her only chair to watch television. Finally, it was noon, time for her to go down to the church for a hot lunch. In the afternoon, she would watch television soap operas, or perhaps spend an hour or two visiting with the many other widows in the hotel.

All the while, uncertainty gnawed at her. Already she was paying over half of her small retirement and welfare income for rent; and if the rent went up any more she would be unable to stay. The hot lunch, sponsored by the federal government, cost her only fifty cents and helped a little. Nevertheless, due especially to medical bills, she frequently ran out of money before the end of the month. Her ulcer was her biggest worry. A few weeks earlier, it had started to bleed, and she had passed out. She had lain helpless for some time before finally managing to crawl to the phone. The desk clerk and some friends had then helped her get to the hospital. She had been more fortunate than some of the others in the hotel. Their lives had ended in their rooms because they had been too weak from malnutrition to crawl for help.

Does this story read like a piece of sentimental fiction? It might, but it is an only-too-accurate account of a retirement dream turned nightmare.[1]

Throughout the centuries, some primitive tribes have abandoned their enfeebled old. The Siriono of the Bolivian forest, for example, simply left them behind as they moved on in their nomadic quest for food. The Hopi, Creek, and Crow Indians constructed special huts away from the village where they abandoned them to die. The Eskimos left them in snowbanks, on ice floes, or forced them to paddle away in a kayak, never to return.

Americans might consider such behavior barbaric. But do we treat our enfeebled old any better? Don't we too frequently simply abandon them in a similar way and for a similar reason? They have become a burden, so we apply the adage, "out of sight, out of mind." We do not see their suffering, nor experience the agony of their lonely deaths. To view our treatment of the elderly in such a way is shocking to us, for we prefer to think of ourselves as kind people, inclined toward charitable works. But does the reality of our treatment of the elderly, the healthy as well as the enfeebled, reflect some hidden dark side of our collective personality? Or is it that social conditions and rapid social changes have had unanticipated consequences that we are only now beginning to comprehend?

Why Is Old Age a Problem Today?

The high value we place on health and the preservation of human life, coupled with certain economic developments and goals, has placed us in the unhappy position of creating a large elderly population with little practical use to society. The natives of the Fiji Islands had no such problem, because they believed a man lived eternally in death at the age at which he died. To assure themselves of healthy bodies for the next life, they would voluntarily kill themselves before they became decrepit.

Americans would look with horror upon the suggestion that our elderly do away with themselves when their economic usefulness or physical health has declined. Instead, we encourage the application of medicine's rapidly expanding arsenal of life-prolonging technology and procedures to save and extend the lives of older people. Pacemakers prod weary hearts. Drugs, surgery, and sometimes machines assist other poorly functioning organs. And now it seems possible that we may be able to replace old organs altogether, with transplants. In many cases, these efforts extend the length of time during which useful and rewarding lives may be enjoyed. Sometimes, unfortunately, they merely prolong a painful life. Who would have believed decades ago that the rapid advancement of modern medicine could ever contribute to anything but the well-being of those whose lives it touched?

The improved care of expectant mothers and newborn infants has reduced the infant mortality rate, allowing an increased proportion of those born to live to old age. Medical advances, including the spread of such public health practices as sanitation, have increased the life expectancy of Americans from forty-nine years in 1900 to seventy years in 1974. Until recently, the birthrate continued to rise, keeping the *proportion* of old people in our society fairly stable. Nevertheless, the *number* of elderly has increased from just over three million in 1900 to over twenty million in 1970. Now our birthrates are beginning to decline. And as the years pass, an ever-increasing proportion of our population will be old. In 1900, only 4 percent of the population was over sixty-five. In 1970, the figure was 9.6 percent. The most common projections for the year 2000 are between 11 and 12 percent, but some suggest that by then the proportion of the population over sixty-five may be as high as 30 percent.

Thus, Americans have saved and enlarged a portion of the population that many other societies through lack of knowledge or desire have allowed to decline. Unfortunately, we have thus far been less successful than many primitive societies in finding something important or satisfying for the old to do. Often, in primitive and earlier societies, the old were respected by and useful to their people to a much greater degree than is the case in our own modern society. Industrialization and the consequent division and specialization of labor, coupled with the growth of modern science, have robbed the old of much usefulness to modern society.

Prior to industrialization, land was the most important source of power. The older people were usually the owners of the property, and therefore controlled much of the economic and political power. This gave them considerable status in the community and in the family. As industrialization spread,

HARPER'S WEEKLY, JANUARY 5, 1861

In earlier times, older people often held economic power through land ownership and were usually treated with a great deal of respect by their families and others.

fewer and fewer people made their living from landed property. Today, few people own land other than the lots on which they live. Most people earn their livings on the job market in return for their services and labor. There are, of course, some older people who control large amounts of money or capital and thus exert considerable power. But the vast majority of old people are not so fortunate; and having no land, no money, and no salable labor, they are comparatively lacking in power and status in the community and in their families.

In earlier societies, the knowledge that the old possessed was often extremely valuable. They preserved and transmitted the culture of the people and the history of the family. Their lifelong experiences enabled them to help assure adequate harvests and to pass on knowledge of a practical and craft-like nature. But as the use of books became widespread, old people became less valuable as storehouses of records and culture. With the advance of scientific research and the rapid development of technology came a decline in the value of the old person's practical experience. So rapid has been the information explosion that the knowledge of older people often has been hastily judged to be "old-fashioned" and therefore useless. Today, those who have a corner on specialized knowledge—doctors, for example—have power based on this knowledge and their related skills. The elderly often lack the more modern specialized knowledge that commands respect and power.

Efforts to increase efficiency have led to the development of highly specialized work roles. This trend, too, has placed the older person at a disadvantage. As an individual's coordination, stamina, sight, hearing, and quickness of thought decline, he is less able to compete. There is some evidence that indicates that the old could do many tasks as well as younger people, if a little more slowly. But minimizing performance time is considered essential to increased production and efficiency.

The maintenance of both a high rate of employment and a fairly stable wage-price structure is a major goal of our society. However, one of the most effective ways of stabilizing wages is to reduce the size of the labor force. This keeps the supply of labor closer to actual demand. Two important social patterns have emerged for keeping the work force reduced to a level in line with demand: a longer training period for the young before they can enter the work force, and retirement. In many occupations, the supply of labor nevertheless is beginning to exceed demand. Among the efforts to remedy this oversupply is the encouragement of ever-earlier retire-

HARPER'S WEEKLY, NOVEMBER 26, 1870

Prior to industrialization and planned obsolescence, older people could continue to work as long as they wished. Many knew trades such as tinkering—the repairing of pots and pans.

ment. But forced retirements often create psychological and financial burdens that the retirees, many of whom are still quite vigorous, must usually face without much preparation or assistance.

It is not surprising, then, that the social role of the elderly is currently unclear and in transition. For a person who has always filled a clearly defined role—as a student, a mother, or a foreman, for example—the amorphousness of the role of retiree or widow can be emotionally disturbing. While America has developed educational and other institutions to prepare the young, it has not evolved comparable institutions to serve older Americans. Preparation for old age is pretty much left up to the individual. Organized roles suitable for and designed to bring satisfaction to the aging are largely nonexistent in our society.

How Has the American Experience Contributed to the Problem?

Americans' ability to prolong life and our emphasis on industrial efficiency are by no means unique in the modern world. Most contemporary industrial societies share these traits. As a result, the aging are also a "problem" to some extent in other industrial societies. But somehow in our society the problem seems greater. Why might this be? Why do we in the United States seem to fear aging and old age more than people in most other societies? Why are we so pleased when someone guesses our age to be younger than it actually is? And why do we abhor wrinkles, gray hair, and baldness?

Perhaps our idolization of youth is connected with the fondness we have always had for the new, as opposed to the old. We prided ourselves on being

CARL FISCHER

This photo exaggerates only slightly the lengths to which older people may feel they must go to look younger and therefore more acceptable.

the "New World," and taught the children of our immigrants to reject the ways of the "Old World." We named states New York or New Mexico, and politicians attempted to popularize political programs by calling them the New Deal or the New Frontier.

Not only have we been the "New World"—we have also always been a society on the move, both geographically and socially. The famous early nineteenth-century French commentator on America, Alexis de Tocqueville, noted this when he wrote, "In the midst of the continual movement that agitates a democratic community, the tie that unites one generation to another is relaxed or broken; every man there readily loses all trace of the ideas of his forefathers or takes no care about them."[2] The opportunity for mobility in the United States has led the young to pay less attention to the ideas, wishes, and needs of their elders. Young Americans have been more able than those in most other countries to establish lives separate from the lives of their parents. This independence of children from parents and parents from children characterizes the relationship between aging parents and their children in America.

Perhaps as a result of our having been a frontier society for so long, our mobility has been accompanied by an emphasis on action and energy. In any case, we like to think of ourselves as an energetic, dynamic people, as a nation of doers. John Kennedy symbolized for many the energy and vigor we like to think of as typically American.

Even before the Civil War, these national characteristics were influencing the lives of older people. Yet the status of the elderly was in general better then. (See Reading 1.) How do we account for this? Certainly, the continued emphasis on industrialization and technological efficiency since the Civil War is part of the reason for the decline of the status of the old. Industrialization also increased the emphasis upon several beliefs that were not indigenous to America, but found their strongest expression here. One was the idea expressed so well by Benjamin Franklin: that hard work was noble and idleness the contrary. The other was the belief in competition, which was reinforced by Darwin's idea of the struggle for existence and the survival of the fittest.

In a society that emphasized the nobility of work and the dangers of idleness, the retiree was of little value to himself or others. And our belief in competition and social Darwinism contributed further to the decline in the position of the elderly by preventing us from cushioning some of the economic blows they would suffer. Until 1935, there was no social security, and pension plans were even more inadequate than they are today. (See Reading 2.) The reasoning of the time went that in the land of opportunity everyone had the same chance to "make it" in open competition. If the retiree found himself impoverished, it was because of some moral flaw; he had not worked hard enough in saving for his old age.

After World War I and the Russian Revolution, this argument gained strength from the fear of socialism. It took the Great Depression to temporarily overcome this anxiety. But although Social Security legislation was passed in 1935, continuing fear delayed until recently the adoption of other measures to help the elderly, such as national health insurance.

When Is One Old?

Americans often smile when they hear about members of primitive cultures who do not know how old

AGING, AUGUST 1972

The two centenarians pictured here are celebrating the woman's 102nd birthday. In our culture, longevity is treated more as a curiosity than as a mark of distinction.

they are. Chronological age, the number of years since birth, is very important to us. Our progress through society is governed by how many years we have been alive. We have to be "old enough" to go to school, drive a car, get a job, or vote.

Our society seems to have selected age sixty-five as the beginning of old age. In the following pages, "elderly" usually implies those over sixty-five. But the primitives may be closer to the truth than we are, because among many tribal societies "old age" is more likely to be determined by physical and mental condition than by how many years have been lived. Everyone is not in the same physical and mental condition at age sixty-five. It is absurd to treat all Americans, especially all workers, as if they immediately become decrepit toads as they blow the candles out on their sixty-fifth birthday cakes. We would do well to consider imitating the primitives and use biological and psychological conditions, rather than age, as our means of determining when one is old.

The process of aging is called *senescence.* Senescence is not the same as senility, which is a vaguely defined pathological condition that includes a variety of physical and behavioral abnormalities, such as loss of self-control and neuroticism. People under sixty-five can be senile and a great many people never become senile at all. There is some evidence that senility is due to arteriosclerosis (hardening of the arteries) rather than to aging. Senescence, however, is the normal process of change in the body that accompanies aging.

The body begins to age almost as soon as it stops growing. The visible signs of aging include the appearance of wrinkled, rough skin with dark spots; dry, thin hair; and stooped or shortened posture from compressed spinal discs.

As one ages, the skin, blood vessels, tendons, and connective tissue lose their elasticity. This is the reason for the hardening of blood vessels and the stiffening of joints. A great many of the physical problems associated with senescence are the result of the general decline of the circulatory system. The heart pumps less effectively, and reduced blood supply impairs mental acuity, interferes with balance, and reduces the effectiveness of the muscles and body organs. Worst of all, the probability of heart attacks and strokes increases.

Circulatory problems aside, as one ages the muscles lose their strength so that endurance and coordination become more difficult. The lungs, kidneys, and other organs also decline. Brain functions decline, though less dramatically. Happily, the degree to which one's body loses its vitality over the years can be influenced by the way one lives. People who have been physically and mentally active throughout their lives remain more vigorous and alert in their later years. It is not unusual for old people to remain mentally bright right up to the ends of their lives.

The world looks, sounds, and tastes different to the elderly. The yellowing lens in the eye filters out the blue, violet, and green spectrum of colors, so that a room decorated in blues and greens could seem drab and gray. It is easier to see the bright colors—yellow, red, and orange. The lens also stiffens, making it harder to focus the eye. Because only one-third as much light enters the older person's eye, he needs brighter light to read and work by.

As senescence proceeds, hearing declines; higher frequencies become inaudible. It takes only a mild deterioration in hearing acuity to make speech diffi-

AGING, FEBRUARY-MARCH 1973

Although this man is seventy-five years old, he still makes it a point to keep in shape by running. Many physical capabilities can be maintained in old age.

cult to interpret. Hearing difficulties are the most prevalent disability among the elderly.

Food may not taste the same to the old person, either. With only one-sixth as many taste buds as younger people, the elderly tend to prefer more seasoned, tarter foods. Touch is less sensitive too.

The aging body is not an insensitive body, however. There is still plenty of ability to enjoy life—if there is something to enjoy. As Morton Puner observes: "Bifocals, hearing aids, canes and all—when away from the drabness of 'normal' old age, they will be as excited and lively, and as noisy, as teen-agers on a spree. . . . An older pleasure seeker makes up for sensory loss by greater emotional response, his appreciation heightened by maturity and the fact that he knows his time is short and that there is so much beauty and novelty still to be shared."[3]

The changes in mental abilities attributed to aging do not invariably occur. Many young people exhibit some of the same mental limitations presumably reserved for the old. Older people may have difficulty forming abstract concepts, but so do many college-age students. On the average, however, the elderly do have greater difficulty learning new concepts, and may take longer to learn. But this difficulty may be partly explained by conditions such as boredom or loss of sensory acuity that make it more difficult for older people to pay attention. It is true, too, that depression and stress at any age can make learning and remembering difficult.

The loss of memory among the aging is widely observed, although it does not affect very much the capacity to retain rote learning or long-term memories, or to perform tasks such as knitting. It has been suggested that there may be neurochemical differences in the way that short- and long-term memories are stored by the brain and that these account for older persons being able to recall clearly details from their childhoods, while forgetting where they have put their glasses. But others have pointed out that past events are more important to the elderly as they evaluate their lives and try to maintain their self-respect than memories of their current, often humiliating, experiences. Consequently, older people may seem preoccupied with the past. Events of twenty years ago may possess greater reality for them than those of a dreary yesterday. There may be remarkably little decline in the mental ability of those who have routinely used symbols and analytical thought throughout their lives. Unfortunately, much of the decline in our old people's mental capacities is probably a direct reflection of the conditions in which we require them to live.

Sexuality is equated with youth. Sad jokes are made about the presumed difficulties of sex among oldsters. Here again, the difference is overstated. Masters and Johnson feel there is no reason that mutually rewarding sexual activity cannot be enjoyed by elderly couples. The amount and kinds of sexual activity one enjoys tend to stay the same throughout life. If sexual behavior declines, it may be more for social than for physical reasons. The most important deterrents to sexual activity in old age, according to Masters and Johnson, are the unavailability of a partner; boredom with one's partner; overconcern with career; overindulgence in food and drink; previous attitudes toward sex, such as Victorian beliefs that sex is inappropriate for older people; fear of poor performance; poor physical and/or mental health; and attitudes toward menopause.[4] (See Reading 3.)

Thus, with sex as with physical and mental capacity, no dramatic decline need take place overnight at age sixty-five or at any other age. We are all gradually aging throughout our lives, and the rate at which we age, and how well we function physically, mentally, and sexually, depends on many factors. While it seems necessary at times to generalize about the physical attributes and behavior of those over sixty-five, we should constantly realize the dangers inherent in doing so, and make every attempt to avoid stereotyping. (See Reading 4.)

How Poor Are the Elderly?

Money is the single most important factor in determining the life-style of older Americans. Without adequate funds, they find it difficult to eat properly, find adequate housing, obtain proper medical care, take advantage of recreational opportunities, travel, or maintain their dignity and independence. While some of the elderly are financially able to enjoy their last years in reasonable comfort, money is a matter of constant concern for most of our old.

While estimates vary, an acceptable minimum annual income has been said to be between $1,500 and $2,000 for a single person, and $2,500 to $3,000 for a couple. But an income in this range only barely pays for necessities and will be completely inadequate for handling such contingencies as replacing or repairing broken appliances, or paying medical bills. Based on this, about one-fifth of people sixty-five and over are living in poverty. In 1973, the Bureau of Labor Statistics estimated a modest budget for a couple would be $5,000 per year. Half of the elderly couples have incomes below even this very modest figure. And nearly 70 percent of the single elderly have incomes below $3,000 per year.

Single people are more likely to be living on inadequate incomes than married people. Most of the single elderly are women, usually widows, living alone or with nonrelatives. The difference between white people and blacks or other nonwhite people is striking. The income of elderly blacks runs about half that of whites. And for Indians it is even less. By one estimate around 90 percent of the elderly black females who are single live in poverty.

Being able to continue working makes a crucial difference in an elderly person's income. The average income for married couples who work, even though usually at low-paying jobs, is about twice that of couples living on social security. In 1973, only 16 percent of those over sixty-five, mostly men, were in the labor force. Loss of work is the single most important source of reduction in income. At retirement, one can expect income to decrease by half. Unhappily, older workers have a hard time getting work of any kind once they retire or are laid off, even if they are still healthy and able to work. For Indians, blacks, and members of other minority groups—people who have had difficulty obtaining jobs throughout their lives—the prospects are dismal.

We have been frequently told that if a person saves and invests carefully while working, he or she can expect a secure old age. However, this is true only if events beyond a person's control do not undo all of his or her efforts. Inflation and increased taxes may erode savings; a long bout with a chronic illness can wipe out the savings so painfully accumulated over the years.

It is true that many elderly people own their own homes. But the equity in a house is not easily con-

GOOD NEWS FOR LATER LIFE

Although this skilled laborer has probably contributed to a pension plan for most of his working life, he may find himself ineligible for pension benefits when he retires.

verted into cash during emergencies, making it a poor contingency reserve. And many of the houses the elderly own are dilapidated and in decaying urban areas, making them less valuable. The houses of blacks and members of other minority groups are even more likely to be in this condition and are often of little commercial worth. Home ownership can also limit the alternative life-styles the older person is willing to explore. However, the psychological security of having a place one can call one's own is worth the cost to many. Aside from home ownership, the majority of people over sixty-five have less than $1,000 in assets. It is a source of considerable dismay that many state governments require an elderly person to have very low income, show that his children cannot provide needed funds, and sign over control of their property through liens in order to receive financial assistance.

Pensions are a great disappointment to many older Americans. Most workers are still not covered by pensions. Retirement programs are concentrated in larger firms and organizations. Small businesses and low-status occupations are sparsely covered, if they are covered at all. As recently as 1965, only one-third of the labor force was covered. Even so, only around 5 percent of the income received by the elderly in America comes from private pensions. As of 1973, there were still so many conditions of eligibility for pension payments that most who contributed to a pension plan never collected. Pension rights were usually not transferable from one company or occupation to another. To qualify, a worker had to have been steadily employed by one organization for a specified length of time before he reached retirement age. If he were laid off, fired, or died before reaching that age, he lost his benefits. If his

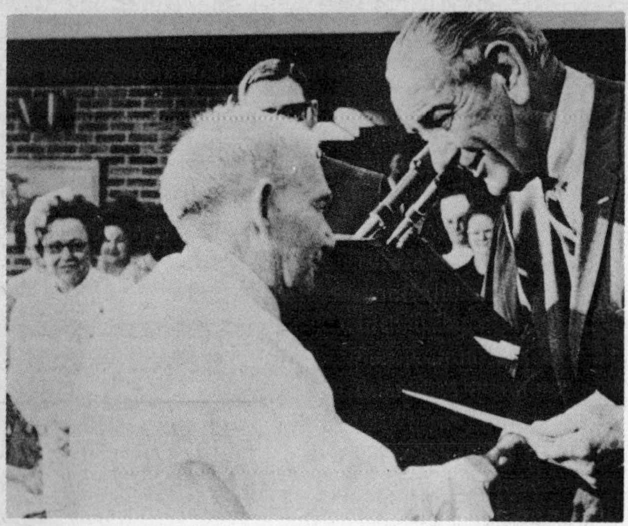

AGING, MAY 1968

President Johnson presents a Social Security check to an older American. Social Security is the chief source of income for most elderly people.

company went out of business or his department were abolished, he was out of luck. And even if he met all of the requirements, the pension fund might have been so poorly managed that he received less than he was entitled to. Needless to say, companies did not always clearly spell out to their workers all of the obstacles that had to be cleared before a full pension could be received.

In 1974, Congress passed a pension reform bill that may lead to effective correction of many of these obstacles. Guarantees of all or part of one's pension money in case of company failure or if one must leave his job before retirement age are among the prominent improvements.

The lowest proportion of the elderly person's income—about 1 percent—comes from cash contributions from his family. But these figures are somewhat misleading, because many children try to provide other types of help, such as transportation, food, care when ill, and home repairs. It must be remembered, however, that many children of old people are themselves getting old. A woman in her eighties may have children who have just retired.

By far the most important source of income for American old people—in terms of both amounts and reliability—is Social Security. Over one-third of the income of the elderly comes from this source, and nearly one-half of our elderly have no other source of income. Social Security benefits have recently been increased. Supplemental payments will be made to keep all old people over sixty-five at a minimal standard of $130 per month. In the future, we can expect Social Security benefits to increase, but they will probably never provide a level of living much above subsistence. While a great many elderly people do not receive public assistance in the form of such things as food stamps and welfare payments, such assistance does contribute between 10 and fifteen percent of all the income received by the elderly.

The biggest difference in spending patterns between those elderly living at subsistence levels and those with larger incomes appears in the amount and quality of food they buy. The elderly poor are more likely to have a high-starch, low-protein diet—exactly the opposite of what they need. Most of what the elderly buy are essentials.

As if the elderly did not have enough problems stretching their dollars, they also suffer as victims of business fraud—housing repair rackets, invest-

JOHN McENROE

Clothes designed with agile young bodies in mind may present difficulties for aging people handicapped by arthritis or other physical ailments.

ment schemes touted as giving much higher interest rates than conventional investments, and worthless retirement properties often steal the elderly person's money. Only now is the government beginning to regulate some of the bigger land development companies by establishing guidelines. The elderly may also suffer financial loss at the hands of medical quacks. And, in an effort to reduce the burdens of their deaths on their families, some elderly people put money into dishonest prepaid-burial programs.

Even legitimate businesses, in their headlong rush for mass market sales, shortchange the elderly. (See Readings 5 and 7.) For example, buttons and zippers on the backs of blouses are difficult to handle with arthritic hands. The print on packages may be too small for the elderly person to read. The amount of food in a package or can may be more than the elderly person can conveniently use.

What Are the Medical Cares of the Old?

Along with sufficient income, good health is the older person's most valuable possession. For it is poor health that leads to the worst things that happen to the elderly: loss of jobs; withdrawal from social roles such as church activities; moving to nursing homes; inability to enjoy available recreation facilities; and, finally, the draining of financial resources by extended medical attention. Over 75 percent of those who are sixty-five years old have at least one chronic (long-term, persistent) condition or disability, such as arthritis. While over one-third of the elderly are restricted to some degree by these conditions, only about 15 percent are disabled to the point where they cannot take care of themselves. Surprisingly, the elderly do not seem

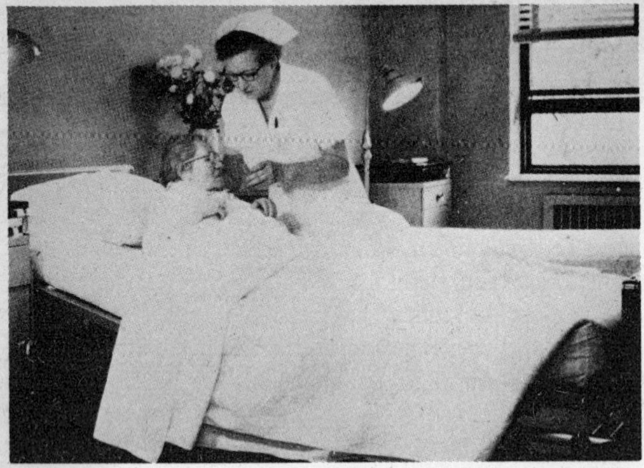

GOOD NEWS FOR LATER LIFE

The elderly fear that ill health will bring with it not only pain and suffering, but dependency as well. Dependency becomes especially crushing when it reaches the point at which the older person's family can no longer provide the necessary care.

to get as many acute (short-term) communicable illnesses, such as the flu, as younger people do, but they do take a little longer to recover from them when stricken. Due in part to a lifetime of poorer medical care, elderly blacks and Indians die younger and suffer more illnesses than whites.

Aging brings with it many disabilities, as we have described earlier. Virtually all of them can be aggravated by stress. It may turn out that many of the diseases of the elderly are less the consequence of aging than of the stressful social conditions we thrust upon them—conditions that could produce disease in people at any age.

Poor nutrition is a serious health problem for the elderly. They need a high-protein, low-fat diet that will prevent fatigue and swelling of joints and will keep up their resistance to disease. But a high-protein diet is expensive and beyond the means of many elderly people. The loss of teeth also causes problems. The aging may be forced to turn to quickly prepared and easily chewed foods that are less nutritious. Aggravating the problem is the fact that many elderly people living alone are not interested in fixing good meals because they have no one to eat them with.

The lack of cheap and reliable public transportation also contributes to the poor health of the elderly. Without it, it is more difficult for those living in their own homes or apartments to get to medical facilities, to shop carefully for food, or even to take advantage of hot-meal programs.

Health and income are closely intertwined. If one is healthy, one is more likely to be able to work and will have fewer medical bills to deplete one's funds. Poor health drains resources and forces the elderly to become dependent upon their families, creating the very situation most dreaded by older people.

There is a serious gap between the medical needs of the elderly and the services that are available. Improved sanitation and nutrition, and the development of drugs and vaccines, has shifted America's primary medical problems from acute illnesses, such as measles and smallpox, to chronic ones, such as cancer and coronary heart disease. But the elderly today still die from pretty much the same diseases the elderly died from in 1900. Heart disease is the most common cause of death among the elderly, followed by cancer and stroke. Influenza and pneumonia are also frequent causes of death.

Unfortunately, our medical-care systems are still primarily geared to treating acute illnesses. They

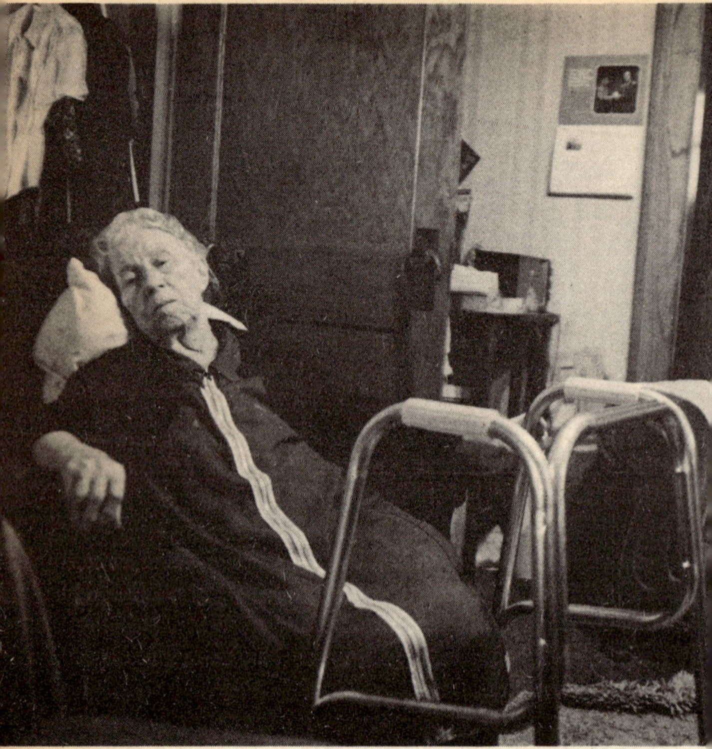

JOEL DAVIS

Cancer is a terrible thing to endure at any age, but the severe debilitation it causes is particularly demoralizing to older people.

have not made the adjustment to the long-term care needed to treat the chronic illnesses suffered increasingly by Americans of all ages. This hits the elderly hard. Chronic-care facilities in hospitals are not expanding at an impressive rate. The development of chronic-care facilities, such as convalescent centers and nursing homes, is being left to private enterprise, as was the case with abortion clinics. Speech, occupational, and physical therapists for heart attack and stroke patients are in short supply. Chronically ill patients are usually required to leave the hospital after their initial hospitalization and move to convalescent centers or nursing homes.

As a rule, insurance programs limit the number of consecutive days in a year they will pay for treatment and the number of dollars that can be spent on a particular illness. Chronic illnesses do not heed the calendar and persist day after day, year after year. Medicare (national health insurance for older people) will pay as long as the patient is in the hospital, but frequently will not pay for nursing-home care. In 1971, only 43 percent of old people's medical bills were paid for by Medicare, and the proportion of the medical bills being paid by Medicare is actually going down. A second national health program, Medicaid, provides help to the indigent poor of all ages. The elderly qualify for Medicaid only if their income is very low. However, if they are eligible for Medicaid, their premiums for Medicare and the deductible amount for certain services under Medicare are paid by Medicaid. Medicaid will also pay for some services and nursing-home care that Medicare does not cover. Even so, because of the extreme expense of being institutionalized with a chronic illness, a large proportion of elderly patients in nursing homes and similar facilities are on welfare. Unbelievably, some of the proposed national health insurance programs considered by Congress in 1974 would not provide significantly improved long-term medical care benefits.

The inability or unwillingness of American society to effectively respond to the medical problems

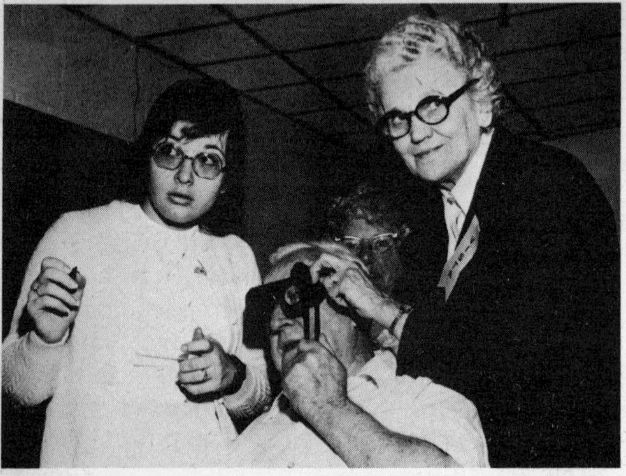

INTERACTION, MARCH 1974

The older man here is receiving an eye test through a VISTA program that promotes early detection of eye disease among the elderly. Becoming blind is one of the greatest fears of the aged, but blindness can almost always be prevented if eye disease is caught and treated early.

of the elderly forces many older people to resort to their families, self-medication, or less expensive quasi-medical practitioners for care, or to go without. The problem is even more serious for blacks and Indians and other minority group members who have suffered a lifetime of indignities and severely overcrowded medical facilities. It is small wonder they are reluctant to use such medical services as are available and rely more heavily on home remedies.

How Do Family, Work, and Other Social Roles Change?

In the United States, many of the roles we play are determined by our age. Retiree, grandparent, senior citizen, and nursing-home resident are some of the roles older people play. Widowhood is much more common among older people. Other roles, such as parent, consumer, and citizen, change as one moves into old age. None of the roles reserved for the elderly are as attractive or as able to excite anticipation as the educational, occupational, and family roles lying ahead of younger people. A small array of poorly defined, low-status roles is all we leave for them.

Family and Friends

Married elderly people are much better off as a rule than single old people. Unfortunately, the longer life span of women has left more than half of them without mates.

The relationship between a husband and wife who have lived together a lifetime and have raised a family changes as they move into old age. They now have much more time for and are more dependent upon each other. Some marriages cannot handle this increased togetherness, but those that can become the major source of contentment to both partners. The understanding wife can be enormously important in helping her husband adjust to retirement. The understanding husband can help his wife adjust to a new role when all the children have left home. A good marriage, or a remarriage, provides the elderly person with companionship and emotional support, sex, the promise of care if he is sick, a focus for daily activities, and frequently greater financial independence. Sex roles often blur, and the husband actively helps in household chores.

Whether or not an elderly widow or widower remarries depends not only upon his or her health and financial situation, but also upon the approval

OF EVERY 100 OLDER PERSONS

SEX

There are 135 older women to every 100 older men. The ratio increases from 120 at age 65 through 69 to more than 160 at age 85 and older.

MARITAL STATUS

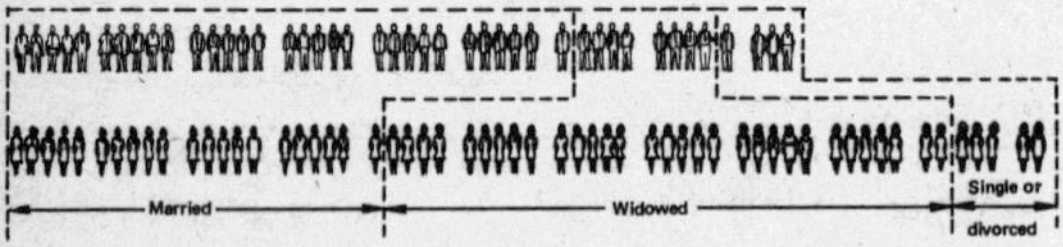

Most older men are married; most older women are widows. There are almost four times as many widows as widowers.

LIVING ARRANGEMENTS

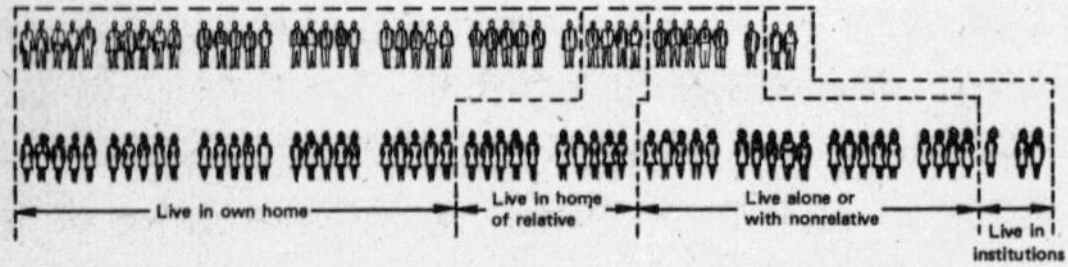

Seven of every ten older persons live in families; about a quarter live alone or with nonrelatives. Only one in 20 lives in an institution. Three times as many older women live alone or with nonrelatives as older men.

(Each figures represents 200,000 older people)

of the families involved. Approval from children and brothers and sisters is as important to the success of the remarriage as parental approval is for younger couples. But sometimes children see a parent's new spouse as an intruder upon the memory of their lost parent and withhold approval of the remarriage.

People who have been single all their lives, particularly if they have always been loners, have little trouble living alone when they are elderly. Those who have been married and are accustomed to very active social lives find the reduction of roles, the loss of loved ones, and the isolation of their later years more traumatic.

Elderly parents and their grown children get along best when both parents and children are independent and self-supporting. Our society emphasizes this independence as a prime quality of adulthood. Both the parents and children expect to treat each other as adults and to live their lives without the other's meddling. Most elderly parents have children living near them who are, with other relatives, their most frequent visitors. Most children and parents expect to have a rewarding relationship with each other throughout life, and the children fully expect to provide attention and some care for their parents. While the financial aid children give parents is not significant, they can give a considerable amount of assistance in other ways. Indeed, the small proportion of elderly people who actually become institutionalized is a reflection in part of the efforts that families make to care for their aging parents as long as possible. Usually it is only when the family feels it can no longer continue such aid that the elderly end up institutionalized.

For children, the needs of their aging parents

BILL GANZEL

The generation gap can produce real feelings of distress and confusion for older people as well as for younger ones.

can present some painful dilemmas. The children may have families of their own putting a heavy burden on their time and finances. If the children are themselves in their sixties or older, they may be struggling to prepare for their own retirement or living already on the limited budgets of retirees. For children in such circumstances, deciding how to divide their resources can be agonizing. No matter how they cut the pie, they cannot do all the things they want or feel obliged to do for their aging parents, their own children, and themselves. In addition, the same social changes that have contributed to making old age a social problem have also contributed to widening the gap between children and their parents and grandparents. Different attitudes toward marriage and premarital sex, toward occupational achievement and material acquisition, toward drugs, toward religion and its institutions, and toward politics and social institutions often produce disagreements between the young and the old, and sadly, between children and their aging parents.

The role of grandparent is surprisingly not as important to most old people in our society as one might think. The grandchildren are usually not around enough to provide much company, and the differences in interests, energy, and life-style are often too great to bridge. Most elderly grandparents do not have grandchildren who are toddlers—they are at least teenagers. And many teenagers shy away from grandparents as well as from their own parents.

Relationships with their brothers and sisters, on the other hand, can be of considerable importance to an older person. Older people often re-establish and mend their relationships with their siblings. Next to children, siblings are the best prospect for a home and companionship once one has lost his or her spouse.

Widows have special problems. The loss of a husband means not only the loss of companionship and money—a widow must also compensate for being deprived of the opportunity to perform her traditional female role as wife, and for the decline in her social status, which was often a function of her husband's occupation. Nevertheless, widowhood can provide a release from worries and responsibilities, especially if the widow's husband had suffered a lingering illness before death. Because of their great numbers, widows often associate with other widows, so widowhood also becomes an opportunity for renewing old friendships. These relationships, however, are often much less intimate and more transitory than those enjoyed with a spouse.

For older people, family is generally more important than friendship. Men, who are more likely to be married in old age, seem to prefer having acquaintances and associates rather than close friends. People from smaller towns and long-time residents of cohesive urban neighborhoods have the best chance of having many friends in their latter years.

Retirement

Retirement can produce both intense and ambivalent feelings in Americans. In our society we see work as a person's measure, and encourage not only hard work but the very identification of the worker with the occupation—"I am a doctor," "I am a businessman," "I am an engineer," "I am a mailman." At the same time we believe that a lifetime of good hard work should be rewarded by a leisurely old age. As we've seen, financial limitations more often make it an insecure and mean existence. And because the later years provide no exciting new roles to replace the occupational roles lost on retirement, the retiree cannot proudly say "I am a. . . ." Instead he must say, "I *was* a good doctor," or "I *was* a successful businessman." Only by looking back can the retiree find a self-image he or she can be proud of. No wonder the elderly enjoy reminiscing.

The more a person's life revolves around work, the more difficult retirement can be. (Fortunately, it is the professional occupations, the ones the worker is more likely to be deeply involved with, that permit one to continue to work as long as he is able. In law, politics, and medicine, it is not infrequent for people to work into their seventies.)

AGING, JUNE 1967

Many older workers would rather not retire. Services like OVER 60 should be expanded to meet the needs of older people who are still willing and able to work.

Because occupations also involve roles in organizations such as unions, professional associations and businessmen's clubs, retirement means more than loss of a job; it also means a sharp reduction in the number of other group memberships as well. (See Reading 6.)

Retirement for most retirees comes rather suddenly. Retirement may even come sooner than it is expected or wanted due to failing health, reorganization or failure of the company, economic changes reducing the demand for one's skills, or pressures to retire early to make room for younger people.

The older worker, although protected by seniority while working, has a very difficult time finding a new job if he or she is laid off. Some people, upon losing their jobs, find themselves forced to retire while they are in their fifties, because no one will rehire them. Many of these older workers have valuable skills and good ideas, and frequently have less absenteeism and are less likely to change jobs than younger workers. In many cases, their work output can equal that of younger workers. Those jobs an older worker can find usually offer less pay and are less dignified than their former jobs.

When retirement finally comes, it is accompanied by little fanfare and little public notice compared with marriages, graduations, and similar events that mark major turning points in life. If one is not prepared for retirement, or if retirement comes under unfavorable circumstances, it can be traumatic. But it doesn't *have* to be stressful or lead to unhappiness. Many elderly retirees are able to maintain their self-esteem despite the loss of roles.

The more confident retirees are that they will be financially secure, the more attractive retirement will be. Retirement counseling, even when the workers are not particularly enthusiastic about it, contributes to a more successful adjustment. While encouraging developments are emerging in retirement counseling, the United States is a long way from providing all of its workers with adequate guidance to assure a reasonably successful retirement. Estimates of the labor force reached by such counseling run as low as 10 percent. Instruction is needed on money matters, health care, legal problems, housing alternatives, government services, sociopsychological problems of retirement, and rewarding uses of leisure time.

Community and Religious Institutions

While many other groups are easing the elderly out, the churches, synagogues, fraternal organizations, lodges, and patriotic groups, including political parties, continue to provide social opportunities for older people. Religious activity is important to many, especially the black elderly for whom Sunday meetings are sometimes the only social contact in the week. Interest in politics also seems to be higher among the elderly than among younger people.

BILL GANZEL

Many older people find that religious services afford both spiritual comfort and a bit of social life, a chance to meet and mingle with peers.

The role of senior citizen, or "Golden Ager," is one that older people largely avoid. It is not uncommon for an old person to refuse to associate with "those old fogies" down at the senior citizens' community center. Only a tiny proportion, not more than 5 percent, join community old-age groups or clubs.

Where and With Whom Do the Elderly Live?

So much has been heard about nursing homes that we tend to forget that fully 95 percent of the Americans over sixty-five do *not* live in homes for the aged or any other kind of institution. If less than 5 percent of the elderly live in such homes, where are all of the rest of them?

Mostly, they are living alone. Older married couples like to maintain their independence. Nearly 80 percent maintain their own households. They may live in apartments, condominiums, mobile homes, or their own houses, just like anyone else. Nearly half of older widows and widowers, singles, and divorcees also live in their own homes. This means the aging are dispersed throughout the community, and this makes provision for and coordination of public services geared toward them much more difficult. (Concentrations of elderly people may be higher in rural areas where retiring farmers move into the small towns.)

As we have seen, the elderly often live in poor-quality housing. They may find themselves trapped in old, low-value houses needing much maintenance and surrounded by ethnic and racial groups different from their own. The parts of town they live in may be decaying and crime-ridden. (See Reading 7.) However, mobile-home parks, apartment complexes

BILL GANZEL

The older American usually does live in his own home, and this gives him a certain feeling of security, even if he has to pinch pennies to maintain himself.

AGING, FEBRUARY 1968

The eighty-eight-unit Florida apartment complex shown here houses retirees. For many, living where there is a high concentration of older people can alleviate the problems of transportation and loneliness.

and retirement villages catering to the needs of the elderly are springing up all over the country. In a few places, large old homes have been converted into residences where a few elderly people can live as a "family." (See Reading 8.) Many communities for the elderly provide security protection, a social center, perhaps a little help on maintenance, and sometimes a hot meal each day. The more advanced may incorporate architectural improvements to make life easier for the elderly, such as ramps, sturdy hand support fixtures, brighter lighting and colors, door handles that do not require the twisting motion of conventional doorknobs that is so painful for arthritics, toilets and furniture that are easy to get up from, and cabinets and other fixtures adjusted to their generally shorter height. Some of the more ambitious projects may include recreational facilities and programs, and perhaps even small medical clinics. These facilities tend to be expensive, however, and are available to only a limited number of persons.

One of the rapidly growing kinds of housing for those who are healthy and can afford it is the lifetime-care facility, which includes a small hospital wing. One pays a lump sum upon entry—it is often about equal to the price of a condominium—for a suite of rooms. (Tenants may or may not have to pay monthly fees.) In return, tenants get prepared meals, security, various services, freedom to come and go, a place to live, and such medical attention as is required for as long as they live. When a tenant's health fails, the medical staff provides treatment at the facility. Thus, those who can afford it can guarantee their independence for the rest of their lives. But as promising as this arrangement sounds, it remains to be seen if it lives up to expectations. For one thing, after the initial trial period, one usually cannot move out of the facility without forfeiting the payment, which often represents the older person's entire estate. If the particular establishment fails, those living there may just be out of luck.

Such alternatives are all certainly welcome improvements over the dreary retirement hotels described in the first pages of this book. Unfortunately, there are still many single older people, especially widows, living alone under such circumstances. Because of the low incomes of black families, the elderly black woman is even more likely to be living alone in such conditions.

When the aging do not maintain their own households, they most often live in the homes of relatives. Nearly one-quarter of the unmarried elderly and 15

BILL GANZEL

Elderly people in rural areas often continue to work at maintaining their property. This couple may derive income as well as recreation from their beekeeping activities.

percent of the married choose this alternative. The largest number live with an unmarried child, the next largest number with married children—more live with the families of sons than with those of daughters—and fewer still live with brothers or sisters.

The quality of life in their relatives' households varies. Baby-sitting and other chores are frequently expected of them. If, as is often the case, the older person is a woman, there is the potential conflict between the two women of the house. The elderly may feel powerless and even useless, because their children control the purse strings and generally have little respect for the elder's knowledge and opinions.

The rural elderly are better off than their urban peers in this regard, because the rural family engages in more activities as a family. There is less division of labor, by occupation, on the farm, so that both young and old can help with the necessary work. The older people can contribute more and are less of a financial burden than is the case in the city. Their knowledge and skills are more likely to be appreciated.

Whether the elderly live alone or with relatives, transportation is a continuing problem. Sometimes nearby children provide chauffeur services. Some communities have mass transportation services that provide doorstep pickup, but these are frequently too expensive for the elderly to use often. Volunteers provide welcome but unreliable and sporadic transportation. Owning and driving a car is a luxury only the more affluent and physically vigorous can afford. And even if mass transit rates are low, the elderly may have to do considerable hiking to get to the stops. The lack of convenient, cheap public transportation hits them very hard. It does little good for the elderly to live in a community with many cultural, medical, and other services and activities unless they can get to them.

Nursing Homes

For a few elderly people, the day comes when independence is no longer practical, because they cannot take care of themselves, or their families can no longer care for them, and they must move into a home. Sadly, it is estimated that fewer than half of these would have to enter a home if personal assistance and occasional medical care could be provided.

Although only a small percentage of the elderly live permanently in homes, many will spend some time convalescing in them, making nursing homes a billion-dollar industry. A number of large companies, such as Four Seasons, Extendicare Inc., Beverly Enterprises, and Medic-Home Enterprises Inc., have invested hundreds of millions of dollars in chains of homes. Shares of their common stocks are among the more desirable because they are so profitable. The mass market approach characterized by large volume purchasing, quality control, mass construction of standard design, computerization, and modern management techniques that has proved so successful in franchise food chains and discount stores is being extended to nursing homes. Many churches, temples, and unions are also building both nursing homes and lifetime-care centers. And, of course, there are a great many small operations run by a few local businessmen or even a single family in a large house.

Nursing homes are classified according to the kind of care they offer. There are approximately five thousand extended nursing-care centers that provide skilled nursing and medical attention twenty-four hours a day. These may be paid for by Medicare. Such centers often serve patients with chronic illnesses who need extensive medical attention while they convalesce. There are also homes that offer long-term nursing care for the chronically ill or disabled who do not require constant medical supervision. As a rule, about eight hours per day of qualified nursing care is expected. These homes are covered by Medicaid, but not Medicare. And finally, there are residential homes that provide board and room, some nonmedical care (such as help in dressing and in personal hygiene), and some modest

HARPER'S WEEKLY, SEPTEMBER 5, 1891

This sketch of old men at a nineteenth-century Home for Aged Hebrews reminds us that even in those days some older people ended their days in institutions.

nursing attention. Many of these are "mom and pop" operations involving small numbers of elderly people in ordinary houses. In 1970, there were over twenty-three thousand nursing homes of all types in the United States. The more extensive and skilled the medical care given, the more expensive the home. The costs vary considerably from a few hundred dollars per month to well over one thousand dollars per month.

In general there is a prejudice against nursing homes among people of all ages that often colors the elderly person's evaluation of the home, even if it is well run. In an earlier era, hospitals were looked upon with similar distaste. They were places where one went to die and from which few returned. Nursing homes are places not only where the elderly wait to die, but where their suffering is isolated from the view of the general population.

Personal and family resources determine when an older person will enter a home, and the reasons for his doing so may be sociopsychological as well as financial. When the older person's health problems (such as incontinence) or personal needs become greater than the family is willing or able to handle, they will place him or her in a home. Older people without spouses or children, or those who have been living alone, are most likely to be put in a home when poor health and financial troubles set in.

Old people frequently feel that going into a home is the ultimate rejection by family and society. (See Reading 9.) The home can be the last of a long string of setbacks and disappointments. The death rate in homes is higher than it is among people of similar age outside. This reflects the poor health and societal abandonment that put patients in the home as well as the treatment they experience there.

The most common complaint leveled against nursing homes seems to be the lack of well-trained, experienced professional staff. In some states, a nursing-home administrator only needs to be eighteen years old and a graduate of a six-month training course in nursing-home administration. Nurses trained and sensitive to the special problems of the elderly are in short supply. Few homes provide social workers, occupational and physical therapists, or other rehabilitative services. With proper therapy, much of the stroke or heart-disease victim's original physical capacities could be restored; yet fewer than fifteen states require, by law, that a home provide such services, so that even if they are prescribed by a physician the patient may not get them. The low wages paid by homes are part of the problem. Despite the high cost of nursing homes, they do not pay wages competitive with hospitals and clinics;

and once a nurse or therapist becomes proficient, he or she may move to a hospital.

Because nursing homes are profit-making businesses, the effort to maximize profits produces a number of other problems as well. Besides cutting staff and keeping salaries down, a home may feed patients cheap food, such as macaroni, that is high in carbohydrates and fats, and may postpone repairs and improvements on the building and minimize amenities. Homes may overcharge patients for optional services, and for cigarettes, gum, and candy bars. When Social Security and other payments come to the home, the patient is supposed to receive pocket money; thirty dollars per month is typical. Some homes keep this, or it just "disappears." In some cases, homes overcharge purposely to run up bills that they then use to put in claims against patients' life insurance when they die.

The quality of care from both particular staff members and from the institution as a whole is another major source of problems and complaints. There may be much delayed or no response to calls for help. Patients may be left sitting for a long time on bedpans. The staff may harass patients they dislike or consider to be insufficiently docile by purposely doing these things, or by withholding services, isolating them in separate rooms in little-used parts of the building, or forcing them to remain bedridden.

Complaints about physical arrangements are less frequent, but still troublesome. There may be too many people in a room, or not enough floor space. The building may be dilapidated, especially if it is in a rural area. The call light by the bed may be difficult to reach, or its signal may not be visible to the nurses in other parts of the building. The stairs

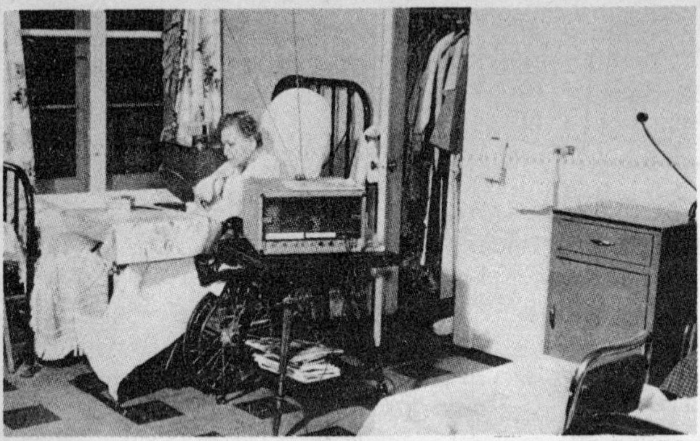

BRIGHTENING THE SENIOR YEARS

Conditions in nursing homes vary widely. This woman at least has some room for her belongings and some space to herself.

may be too steep. Handrails may be inadequate. Toilets and showers may not be conveniently located. About 30 percent of nursing homes are really bad, according to one estimate. Another 40 percent are good, and the remaining 30 percent are reasonably adequate. (See Reading 10.)

Not all of the problems in nursing homes are caused by the owners and staff. Many of the patients also cause problems by stealing, being noisy, and disrupting others' privacy. Some nursing-home residents sleep on their money and valuables to protect them from other residents.

Nursing-home residents often suggest that life would be more pleasant if they could have a chance to invite guests to dinner occasionally, have wine with dinner, have more contact with outside groups, have access to bigger libraries, and have locks on bathroom and other doors (for privacy) and individual thermostat controls. They also suggest that homes would be improved if overly noisy or "confused" patients were prevented from interfering with others' privacy and belongings; if more masculine recreation facilities, such as wood-working shops, could be provided; and if coffee urns were provided so that patients could be gracious hosts to visitors.

What Are the Leisure-Time Activities of the Elderly?

One of the few things the elderly have plenty of is free time. As in every other age group, those old people who have money and health can be quite active. They may travel, play golf, enjoy cultural activities, give parties, and dine out. But because most elderly people have little money, and often not a lot of energy, their recreation is limited to what they can do cheaply and without too much physical exertion.

INTERACTION, JANUARY 1974

Older people who enjoy gardening or some other special activity can put their skills to work for the benefit of the entire community through programs such as RSVP (Retired Senior Volunteers Program).

INTERACTION, JANUARY 1974

By far the most common leisure-time activity is watching television. Interestingly, the elderly are interested less in light comedy than younger people and more in serious programs and the news. After television, favorite hobbies include reading, puttering around in a garden, visiting, going for walks, and working on craft projects. Elderly men often enjoy spectator sports. The elderly may stop going to movies because they are expensive and there are transportation problems.

The leisure-time activities one engages in when one is old are largely determined by what one chose to do when one was younger. Older people are usually reluctant to try something new in which they do not feel competent and for which they may have no real taste. This is one reason retirement counselors encourage people in their forties to take time to learn and develop recreational skills and interests that can be a source of pleasure throughout later years.

Our educational systems have been strained for so long by the increasing numbers of young people that only now, when the post-war baby boom has passed and the birthrate is declining, are we getting the opportunity to consider seriously the educational needs of adults. The concept of lifetime education for all adults is spreading. Special educational programs for the elderly, focusing on their physical and intellectual needs and interests, are emerging, especially in the community colleges. Many colleges and universities are establishing or considering the policy of admitting those over sixty-five under special low-tuition or no-tuition plans. Because most of the elderly are not looking for occupational training, the courses they favor are those that enrich their lives and open new vistas of understanding. Hopefully, the colleges and universities can become oases where older people can gain insights into their situations and develop new skills to enrich life as it unfolds. But education is not yet an important element in the leisure time of the elderly.

People become more similar in the way they spend their days as they retire and grow older. Older men of quite different backgrounds may organize their day around maintenance of their house and yards, similar hobbies, and television.

Because the elderly cannot receive support for their feelings of self-worth from the jobs they no longer have, or from the organizations of society from which they must withdraw, leisure-time activities can be an important source of feelings of worth. A well-made coffee table, a knitted sweater, a beautiful flower garden can be sources of both pleasure and reassurance. Work in volunteer organizations can provide the elderly with meaningful outlets for their energies and talents.

What Is It Like to Die in America?

Death is a constant companion to the elderly. They see their friends and relatives dying, and every funeral is a reminder of their own numbered days. Even so, most do not seem to fear death. Their dread is more often focused on the pain, disability, and long periods of suffering that may precede death. Religious people who believe in an afterlife may have even less fear of death, unless the religion teaches of an afterlife in which horrendous punishments await the sinners.

If asked how they would like to die, many if not most Americans would describe a death with dignity.

They would like to die in their own homes, with mental faculties intact and surrounded by adoring and grateful family and friends. Before modern industrial society reached full bloom, this was usually the way people did die. The family was responsible for providing a place to die and for preparing the body for burial, and in some cases for the burial itself. But now too many Americans die in hospitals or nursing homes, and they are laid to rest by strangers. The family has given up these unsavory tasks to the mortuary and nursing-home industries and to the medical profession.

In the hospitals, great efforts are made to separate the dying and the dead from the living. Dying patients are moved into rooms alone, and orderlies spirit away the bodies during hours when few visitors and patients are around to see. The medical staff routinely shields the dying patient from discovery of his own impending death. Nevertheless, the patients often discover they are dying because they realize they are being treated differently by the medical staff. The nurses and doctors tend to turn their efforts to the patients they have hope of curing, and interaction with the dying patient tends to take on a distant and often falsely optimistic tone. The family, too, begins to treat the patient differently when they know he or she is dying.

A number of writers have pointed out that this whole charade is often unnecessary and may even be detrimental—Elisabeth Kübler-Ross's *On Death and Dying* is one well-known work that advances this view. While there will be some people who cannot handle their own deaths, the majority of people can, especially with the help of their families and clergy.

There are many arguments in favor of treating death openly. Doing so gives the family time to make the necessary arrangements (including financial arrangements) for the death. It provides time and often the incentive to redress old wrongs and heal misunderstandings among relatives and friends. It also provides opportunity for dying persons to prepare for death. They may want time to reassess their lives and to come to some conclusions about what their lives meant and what was accomplished. Often, family members are more distraught than the dying person over the impending death. The dying themselves can help others accept and prepare for the death. Now, we tend to wall the dying off with silence; we often require them to die alone. And the living must struggle with their loss, as they will struggle with their own deaths, pretty much alone.

The dominant attitude in America is that death is inevitable, but not to be discussed. It is taboo as a topic of conversation just as sex used to be. Many of our young have never even seen a dead body in its natural state. The whole society is structured to prevent death from being disruptive to the larger society. It has been suggested that this may be the reason for mandatory retirement. The increased health problems that accompany aging, especially the severe disruption of large organizations caused by the death of key personnel, make retirement a prudent protection that helps to guarantee the smooth operation of the organization. The placement of the dying in hospitals and nursing homes where they are less disruptive for the family and community is a means of keeping life tidy and orderly, but this is unfortunately often achieved at the expense of the dying.

Is Old Age Ever Pleasant?

For too many of the elderly, the later years are a time of great difficulties. For some, old age is simply a nightmare. For a tiny minority who are wealthy and healthy, old age can be a time of luxurious leisure. But for those of modest means who have been frugal and prepared thoughtfully, old age can be a period, if not of luxury, then at least of reasonable comfort and pleasure.

A couple in good health who own their home outright and have only ordinary upkeep on house and car, who have accumulated through careful nurturance savings of a few thousand dollars, and who receive a Social Security and pension income of between $400 and $500 per month can expect to pass the time quite agreeably. They may have to depend on their children and senior citizens' groups to provide trips and outings. They may have to take advantage of hot-lunch programs. But they still should be able to afford meat frequently, and have enough resources for a few treats.

Those a little better off may find group travel plans within their means. For these, the dream trip to Hawaii or Europe can become a reality. The occasional shopping trip with lunch at a favorite restaurant, a visit to the beauty parlor, and season tickets for the local concert or theater series may spice up their days. They should also be able to afford the latest best-seller and the current rage in arts and crafts. Some of the more enterprising may even start small home businesses focused on their hobbies—they may sell or repair antiques, for example. They should find themselves in a position to enjoy their hobbies and visit their relatives and friends more freely.

Some churches and other organizations have meaningful activities that absorb large amounts of an older person's time, and may even pay him a little. The Mormons, for example, employ hundreds of older people in their temples, where they officiate at sacred ceremonies. Many Mormons look forward to the opportunity to serve in this capacity, although they are not paid. To other elderly people, the retirement years are just a great time to go fishing or to hitch up a trailer and take off to see the country.

Far from being stereotyped in their approach to living, the elderly can be surprisingly resourceful and innovative. Indeed, some observers claim that a greater variety of very original life-styles exist among the elderly than among the young. Some of these life-styles may be deserving of as much attention and imitation as the better-known and much-ballyhooed life-styles of the young. These varied life-styles frequently reflect the practical skills, the wider range of appreciation, and the greater wisdom that comes with a long and fruitful life.

What Is Being Done About the Problem?

The problems of the elderly are entering the public spotlight and becoming a popular cause. Numbers of programs on the federal level and in local communities are being enacted. The federal government has an Administration on Aging, many states have an office on aging, and some counties and municipalities have community councils on aging. Scientists and academicians are becoming very active in the study of aging, and scientific gerontological societies are already active. Government research grants are encouraging the study of the elderly by

AGING, MARCH-APRIL 1969
Courses on gerontology are attracting students both young and old. This group is meeting in a classroom at the University of South Florida.

people in the scientific disciplines and the humanities. More and more centers for the study of gerontology and death are being started and are rapidly filling with students. Subspecialties focusing on gerontology in nursing, social work, medicine, architecture, and many other professions are expanding. Professional nursing-home administration associations are growing. The popular press and newspapers are providing books and articles to educate the public about the problems of the elderly, and a few high schools are beginning to offer courses aimed at helping the young to understand the old. (See Reading 11.)

There are a number of programs, often federally funded and state or locally administered, to provide services needed by the elderly. The Older Americans Act as amended in 1973 is especially to be noted in this regard. To help combat malnutrition, hot-meal

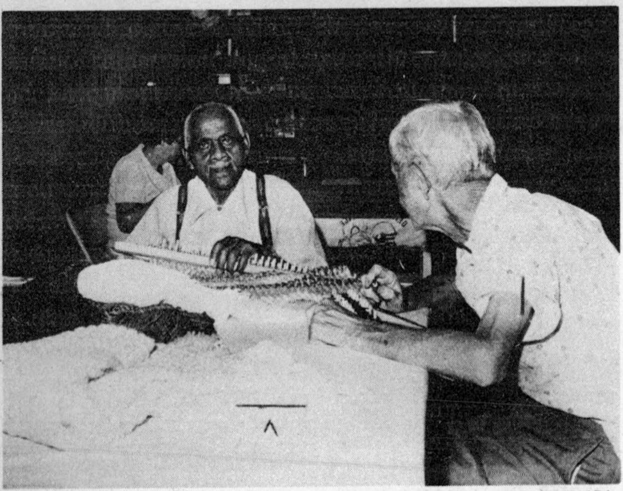

INTERACTION, JANUARY 1974

An RSVP volunteer teaches the nearly lost art of peg knitting to a hospital patient. It is important for older people who retain skills virtually unknown to their children to be able to use and pass along their unique knowledge.

programs have been developed. For nursing-home residents who feel they are being mistreated, there is the experimental Nursing Home Ombudsman Program. In the Michigan version of this program, older citizens volunteer to take responsibility for a particular nursing home in their area. They frequently visit the home and get to know the residents. Any time these residents have a complaint, they can call the ombudsman, who, if he feels the situation warrants it, can notify the head of the program in the state capital. If investigations confirm the complaint, the appropriate state agency can be brought into action against the home.

A great many volunteer programs designed to utilize the considerable knowledge and experience of the elderly are springing up. There is RSVP—Retired Senior Volunteer Program—which tries to match work and service opportunities with the elderly volunteers seeking them. SCORE—Service Corps of Retired Executives—helps small businessmen through consulting. The Foster Grandparent programs pay the elderly about thirty-five dollars per week for twenty hours in which they provide individual attention to needy and ill children and teenagers.

Within local communities, senior-citizen centers, Golden Age Clubs, and similar groups often provide valuable services. Efforts to respond to the reduced income of the elderly have led to reduced fares on public transportation, lower fees for public parks, special rates at places of entertainment, and tax relief. (See Reading 12.)

Despite all of these efforts, the key problems of the elderly have yet to be solved. Most elderly people still need recourse to adequate and reliable income, health protection, transportation, and good living arrangements; and the roles of the elderly must be transformed into roles that both the elderly and society consider significant. Reduced income and increased medical expenses create a pinch that should be eliminated. Without health care and adequate income, the elderly cannot take advantage of the other programs that are provided, no matter how glamorous these may be.

It seems apparent that the kinds of major developments that will have to take place before the needs of the elderly are met are largely going to have to come about through the political efforts of the elderly themselves. These efforts may involve alliances with larger groups, such as unions, or the formation of special interest groups by and for the

JOHN McENROE

An older American promotes "consciousness raising" via the bumper sticker. (Bumper sticker © 1974, Sunrise Sales Corporation, Southfield, Michigan.)

aging. (See Reading 13.) Such political groups are appearing. But even though there are a few "Gray Power" groups, and many well-organized local elderly voting blocs, as a rule the elderly are still fragmented and politically ineffectual. This seems to be due in part to the fact that the issue has only recently been recognized. The lack of funds, the geographical dispersion of the elderly, transportation and communication difficulties, and similar problems also keep the elderly politically powerless. As the elderly move in increasing numbers to central locations where there are high concentrations of older people, such as high-rise apartment buildings and retirement centers, political organization may become more effective.

As our elders rise and demand the honor they deserve but which we always seem to have excuses for not giving them, we may also discover that we are guilty of ageism—prejudice against the elderly. Just as we are learning that black can be beautiful, so we must learn that gray can be beautiful, too. In so learning, we may brighten the prospects of our own old age.

Part Two

Selected Readings

HARPER'S WEEKLY, MARCH 8, 1890

In the early days in America, older people were expected to actively contribute to society as long as they were physically able.

1

Old Age in Colonial America

by JOHN DEMOS

Early in our nation's history, colonists did not have to retire at any specific age. Nevertheless, as the following selection indicates, the frontier conditions of our society worked more to the advantage of the young than the old.

THE MATERIAL on officeholders makes one point immediately apparent: the colonists had little idea of retirement—little, that is, beyond a retirement that was made necessary by illness or extreme infirmity. . . .

* * *

It is easier to measure these careers in public service than to find comparable materials bearing on the *private* pursuits of elderly men. But almost certainly the same basic assumptions prevailed. Samuel Eddy, for example, apparently continued his work as a tailor until quite an advanced age; for in 1678, when he was over seventy, the court was approving money to reimburse him for helping to outfit the colony's soldiers in King Philip's War.[1] More generally, many of the wills written by elderly men imply a direct and exclusive interest in the continuing management of their farms; there would be no change in this situation until the moment of the testator's death. We did note earlier certain cases in which the testator mentioned some particular assistance provided by a child or other relative. But they seem on their own evidence to have been regarded as somewhat exceptional. Often there is explicit reference to the "extreme old age and weakness" of the one party, by way of explaining the need for the solicitude of the other. Clearly similar was the case of the man who conveyed his property to someone else *before* death in exchange for a guarantee of personal care. The reason for such arrangements was presumably the one mentioned by Samuel Nash: "being aged, and not in a capassety to live and keep house of himselfe."[2] Conversely, as long as the "capassety" remained, a man would prefer to hold direct control over his property and direct responsibility for the day-by-day management of his affairs.

Insofar as the culture did propose to distinguish the elderly from the rest of the populace, it emphasized "their long experience, and manifold advantages . . . for the getting of wisdom."[3] The approved

1 *Records of the Town of Plymouth,* I, 151.
2 *Plymouth Colony Records,* VI, 125-126.
3 *The Works of John Robinson,* I, 253.

role for the old man was the dispensing of "counsel" to others, particularly the young. He should, as a consequence, be treated more respectfully; indeed "a bashful and modest reverence" was his due under virtually all conceivable circumstances.

But this sort of stereotype is not worth elaborating in any great detail, since it is still familiar enough today. Rather more important, perhaps, is the whole question of actual *behavior* in this regard. No comprehensive answer can be given, but there are at least some scraps of evidence to suggest that old age brought its own share of difficulties, and its own particular worries, for many people in the old colony. Elderly men, for example, seem to have been no less immune to suits or other actions at court than anyone else. And some of these episodes revealed a deep strain of bitterness that was not muffled by any sense of discrepancy between the ages of the people involved. Consider the following piece of testimony in a case at Scituate in 1685. The chief participants are Nathaniel Parker, age twenty-three, and Edward Jenkins, age approximately sixty-five; the setting is Jenkins' house; and the issue between them is a debt of several bolts of cloth. Parker (as the debtor) declared that "he had noo boults at present without he should stele them for him and that he wold not doo: as sum had dun . . . as soon as nathanell parker had spook these words: edward jenkins tould nathanell parker that hee never brook up elder kings chest and took mony out of it with that nathanell parker ran too edward jenkins and [took] edward jenkins by the color or the neckcloth that was about edward jenkins neck and nathanell parker . . . sayed god dame me if thou wart not a ould man I wold bet they teeth douen thy throt."[4] It seems from this testimony that the two men confronted each other on a footing of equality—if, indeed, Parker's last comment is not meant to express contempt for his adversary's weakness as an "ould man." Certainly, it is quite an uninhibited performance on both sides.

Worst of all, perhaps, for most elderly people was a nagging fear of being ignored or abandoned by those who should be closest to them. This fear shows up in some wills—in the elaborate efforts, for instance, of a dying man to insure that the needs of his widow will be fully met. Occasionally, these arrangements did not work out. When William Clark of Duxbury died in 1687, he willed his entire estate to "william bonny (whom I brought up from his Childhood)," provided that Bonny would continue to live in his house and look after his aged widow, Martha. But scarcely more than a year later, Martha Clark complained to the court that Bonny had left her, and a warrant was issued for his arrest. He was duly apprehended and the will was read to him in the presence of a magistrate. But "he Answered that he would Rather than goe to dwell with her again Renounce his legacy."[5] Certainly this was *not* a typical occurrence: in the great majority

---

[4] Ms. deposition in the "Davis Scrapbooks," III, 8, at Pilgrim Hall, Plymouth, Mass. This quotation is unusually rough and complicated, and may warrant some sort of "translation" into modern usage. With only spelling and punctuation changed, it would read: "he had no bolts at present without he should steal them for him, and that he would not do, as some had done. . . . As soon as Nathaniel Parker had spoken these words, Edward Jenkins told Nathaniel Parker that he never broke up Elder King's chest and took money out of it. With that Nathaniel Parker ran to Edward Jenkins and took Edward Jenkins by the collar or the neckcloth that was about Edward Jenkins' neck, and Nathaniel Parker . . . said 'God damn me, if thou wert not an old man I would bat thy teeth down thy throat.' "

[5] *Pilgrim Notes and Queries*, IV, 4.

of cases, the aged and infirm received whatever care they required from their children (or other kin, or servants). Yet in a land so open and a society so strongly marked by geographical movement, nothing was absolutely assured. There was always the chance that an elderly couple would at a critical moment find itself cut off from any ready source of help—with children settled elsewhere and perhaps not even in touch. A vivid metaphor from Bradford's history provides a final flourish for this picture. Bradford has been describing the whole process of dispersion that removed from the town of Plymouth so many of its finest citizens. But the image he chooses to express his sorrow about this process comes from another, much more personal dimension of experience. The town, he writes, was "like an ancient mother grown old and forsaken of her children, though not in their affections yet in regard of their bodily presence and personal helpfulness; her ancient members being most of them worn away by death, and these of later time being like children translated into other families, and she like a widow left only to trust in God. Thus, she that had made many rich became herself poor."[6]

*   *   *

There is more that can be said—but only in a speculative way, since the relevant evidence has not survived. Very likely, the advantages of young people in terms of adaptability, sturdiness, and resourcefulness were particularly important, and *visible,* in frontier circumstances; and perhaps for this reason, it was unusually difficult to maintain the traditional subjection of youth to age.

---

[6] Bradford, *Of Plymouth Plantation,* 334.

CHARITIES AND THE COMMONS, MARCH 6, 1909

By the beginning of this century older individuals, like this Pittsburgh worker, were increasingly discriminated against.

2

Old and Poor Prior to Social Security

by MABEL LOUISE NASSAU

The following case studies are just a few of those that appeared in a book published in 1915. The work seems to indicate the need for some form of social insurance. But it would not come until twenty years later, after almost all other major countries had enacted such legislation. Many experts believe that today we still lag behind other major nations in our care for the old.

Mrs. C.

MRS. C. is sixty-two years old, and (now that her varicose veins have grown so bad that she can't work) has a little top-floor back room in a furnished-room house, though until recently she received five dollars a week in domestic service. She was a

From *Old Age Poverty in Greenwich Village: A Neighborhood Study*, by Mabel Louise Nassau (New York; Fleming H. Revell Co., 1915).

servant before she married, so she naturally turned to that after her husband died sixteen years ago. He was a mechanical engineer, and died on a trip to Japan, leaving no savings. Mrs. C. has had to stop work before because of illness, and each time her savings have been broken into. This time they are nearly gone, and the visiting nurse told me she probably can never work out again, though she thinks she can begin work again soon. The clergyman of her church thinks she ought to go into a Home, but she refuses to do that. She is independent and cheerful, and doesn't want charity. She is cooking on the oil stove that heats her room just enough to keep her alive, and has perfect faith that she can get a good position again just as soon as she can stand on her feet and hobble around.

Her children are dead, and she has no one to help her. She says she spends $3.50 a week for room, heating, food, etc.

Mr. McI.

Mr. McI. is both typical and unique—typical in that he represents a class of men thrown out of employment, partly by being pushed out by younger men and partly by having a trade that is growing obsolete, and unique because of his present mode of existence and support. He is a native New Yorker, single, aged sixty-seven. He is in good physical and mental condition. I made only one call on him and his sister, but was so entertained I wished to go again. I found her —she is seventy-three—cooking the dinner, and he was sewing on the machine, doing sewing given to his sister by the church. When I asked how he was able to do that kind of sewing, he told me his story. As a young man he had tuberculosis, and when he recovered he could not do heavy work, so he became a woman's dressmaker (not tailor) and followed that trade for thirty-four years. He spoke with pride of dressmaking done for actresses (such minor ones that I failed to recognize their names, but I tried not to show my ignorance). He showed me a waist he had made his sister as a sample of his work, and it was certainly a marvelous creation. But he said, "Nowadays people buy ready-made clothing; it's cheaper." So he gets work only occasionally. He and his sister have two rooms for eleven dollars a month, and she gets three dollars' worth of sewing a week and a gift of fifty cents a week, which probably pays the rent and for her food, and he probably makes enough for his food. And he does most of her sewing. He is said to be a kind, good man, and his pride, though amusing, also has something fine about it—to love work, even if dressmaking work, is to share in the dignity of labor to some extent! He is still proud of his profession and of his figure and his small wrists, and he is bright and cheerful, and he and his sister seem happy together. But if it were not for the church assistance, what would they do?—for neither could really earn money at regular work.

Mrs. McC.

MRS. McC.'s family is not an example of the "worthy poor," but the reverse. The whole family illustrates the degenerating effects of extreme poverty.

Mrs. McC. herself at seventy can scarcely be blamed for not working, but she certainly has lost a great deal of her self-respect. She was born in Ireland and worked in a factory till she was married. Her husband was a weaver in Ireland, and came to the United States for "better wages," but succeeded in becoming only a day-laborer and died twenty-eight years ago. Then Mrs. McC. went out to do scrubbing and washing, and worked till three years ago. Then she had pneumonia and an abscess in her ear, and she is sick and feeble now. Of six children, only two are left, and one cannot help, so she is dependent on a widowed daughter, with whom she lives. This daughter has four children, the youngest in a day nursery. The daughter works out by the day, but isn't successful, making only about eight dollars a month for the rent and a little over. A charitable association provides some groceries. A church helps a little. Mrs. McC. confessed to the groceries, but said they did not have enough to eat, and rather begged for contributions. Afterward, I found that several settlements had helped, sending the children away for vacations and so on, and that the mother was considered worthless. Now all these doles and makeshifts are bad for the family, especially the uncertainty of them, and the temptation is to rely upon them and to try for more aid instead of more work, for apparently the daughter could work more, and the effects are the worst upon her. Of course, old Mrs. McC. can't work, and it is possible to believe that the daughter worked hard years ago. The point of this story is meant to be that sometimes the strain for the middle generation is too great, and that occasionally people succumb, and that after all the individuals who fall are not always entirely to blame when conditions are too hard for them!

Mr. M.

Mr. and Mrs. M. are separated, not through lack of affection, but because the only two of the eight sons and daughters living who can help their parents are two widowed daughters. One widowed daughter supports her father. She does janitress work, for which she gets nice light rooms and ten dollars a month. Then she does scrubbing at some offices, for which she gets twenty dollars a month. But thirty dollars a month clear isn't much to feed two adults and two children and to clothe them and to provide for all emergencies. And she must work very hard to do the office and janitress work! She says her father doesn't realize what a burden he is. He worked on the docks for about ten dollars a week and when incapacitated hadn't saved anything. The old woman lives with the other widowed daughter. I just stumbled on this family when inquiring for someone else. I made two calls on the daughter with whom the old man lives, and one call at the house where the old woman lives—where I saw the old woman, but not the daughter. That daughter goes out cleaning and supports her mother and three children, and an invalid brother lives there too. The old woman gave the impression of living on very short rations and said, "I've just given the children some breakfast, but we didn't even have any sugar for the coffee." So apparently both families are struggling hard.

JOHN McENROE

Contrary to popular opinion, older Americans' interest in sex does not disappear the day they start to collect Social Security. This bumper sticker uses humor to make an important distinction. (Bumper sticker © 1974, Sunrise Sales Corporation, Southfield, Michigan.)

3

Sex and the Senior Citizen

by NORMAN M. LOBSENZ

In the essay that follows, the author examines our culture's unwillingness to take seriously the sexuality of its elderly citizens. He then goes on to point out that not only can they in general still perform sexually, but that, in many cases, very positive physical and psychological effects result from such activity. And if society's attitudes on the question were to change, even more positive effects would probably result.

A WRITER looking for a funny ending to his interview with Bob Hope asked the comedian recently if he thought there was still sex after sixty-five. "You bet," said Hope, "and awfully good, too. [*Pause for a beat of exquisite timing.*] Especially the one in the fall."

The image of geriatric lovemaking seems always good for a laugh. A few years ago, Dr. Mary Calderone, executive director of SIECUS, the Sex Information and Education Council of the United States, and one of the nation's leading authorities on sex education, was answering questions from an audience of Chicago high-schoolers. When one daring teenager asked, "How old are you, are you married, and are you still doing it?" the students broke into giggles. Dr. Calderone was characteristically forthright. When the laughter died down, she said, "The answer to the first part of that question is sixty-four, and the answer to the other two is yes." Then she added, "Young people do not have a monopoly on sexuality. It is with you all your life."

Indeed, every medical study conducted during recent years indicates that there is no physiological reason why older men and women in reasonably good health should not have—and be able to have—an active and satisfying sex life. Yet, despite increasing scientific evidence to the contrary, our culture continues to foster the belief that by the time one is in his or her sixties, sex is neither necessary nor possible. Or if it *does* occur, it is somehow not quite normal. Or that it certainly isn't nice for the old folks to be indulging in it.

In a time of ever more tolerant attitudes toward sexual self-determination for everyone else, why this puritanical approach to "senior citizens"? Some of the reasons may stem from long-dormant Oedipal fears and incest taboos associated with the idea of sexual expression on the part of parental figures, from remnants of childhood's disbelief that one's mother and father—and by extension any older person—actually ever make love. Manhattan psychotherapist Dr. Leah Schaefer reports, for example, that none of the women she interviewed for a book on sex could accept with any equanimity the idea of their own parents engaging in intercourse.

Another source of sexual puritanism toward the aged is the clichés of a youth-fixated society. Given the movie-television-advertising stereotype that sexuality exists only in and for beautiful people with firm flesh and agile bodies, the notion of older persons enjoying it—wrinkles, flabbiness, and all—seems at first ludicrous and then repugnant.

For the twenty million Americans over sixty-five, these attitudes present formidable problems. Having been conditioned to believe erroneously that sexual performance declines to the vanishing point with age, or that sexual exertion is dangerous to their health, many older persons tend to give up sex more or less completely.

Others shut off sexual feelings out of shame and embarrassment about having them. Doctors and counselors report that when older people *do* admit to having sexual desires, they often apologize for having such "undignified" or even "depraved" sensations. Dr. Joseph T. Freeman, a Pennsylvania gerontologist who has written for medical textbooks on the sexual aspects of aging, cites the case of an eighty-four-year-old man who complained to his physician about the frequent demands for intercourse made by his seventy-nine-year-old wife. The husband was able to meet them, Freeman writes, but felt that this activity was "not natural for such an old man and woman." Another couple in their early seventies had continued to make love at least once a day; yet both believed, says Freeman, "that they were doing something unnatural . . . an expression of some abnormal inclination."

Some older people fear the ridicule or censure of

younger persons if they show signs of still being interested in sex. Children and even grandchildren disapprove, make them feel guilty. I was told of a recently remarried seventy-eight-year-old man whose daughter greets him every morning with a derisive "How did it go last night?" A Florida psychiatrist reported two instances where children tried to commit their parents to a mental institution because they had moved in with friends of the opposite sex. It's not just coincidence that we never refer to even the most profligate youth as a "dirty young man," but are quick to label any older person who shows some interest in sex as a "dirty old man." (One California septuagenarian struck back with a bumper sticker on his sports car: "I'm not a dirty old man, I'm a sexy senior citizen.")

The D.O.M. label is applied with even greater vehemence if the aging man or woman is involved with a much younger person, although there's no reason why love or sex should be age-segregated. May-December relationships can and do flourish. It is true that in many such cases the attraction is not necessarily romantic. Younger women often marry older men—and younger men often marry older women—for their money, fame, power, wisdom, or out of neurotic needs.

Yet if this general climate of deprecation hampers sexual expression for married older persons, it creates far greater obstacles for two-thirds of those men and women over sixty-five who never wed or are widowed or divorced. And because of a combination of demographics and cultural standards, women are affected more seriously.

To begin with—thanks to a longer life expectancy, plus the fact that women are usually younger than their husbands—older women outnumber older men.

According to the latest available statistics from the Department of Health, Education, and Welfare, for every one hundred people in the over-sixty-five age bracket, fifty-seven are women. Moreover, two-thirds of them are widows, and there are three times as many widows as widowers. In terms of sheer availability of partners, therefore, older men have a far better statistical opportunity for sex.

Social custom offers men a similar advantage. It's much easier for an older man to find a wife than for an older woman to find a husband (in a typical year, thirty-five thousand such men and only sixteen thousand such women will wed) largely because he retains the male prerogatives. He's more likely to take the sexual initiative. Age is not deemed to make as much difference to his looks. It is more acceptable for him to wed a young wife than for an older woman to wed a young man.

Moreover, *non*marital sex is more available to men than to women. Since one tends to follow in old age the cultural patterns of one's youth, today's over-sixty-fives—who grew up when "illicit" sex was a serious transgression—cannot easily accept the idea of such relationships. Even so, men are still freer to pursue them. Dr. Eric Pfeiffer, head of Duke University's Center for the Study of Aging and Human Development, reports that close to 90 percent of the women interviewed for its long-term study of geriatric sex behavior had stopped having intercourse when their husbands became ill, impotent, or died. "By contrast," reports Dr. Pfeiffer, "marital status had little or no effect on the incidence of sexual activity among elderly men."

The "double standard" he grew up with—permitting greater sexual freedom to men—enables the older man to purchase sex without the guilt or social disapproval that it would create for the older woman. (And from a purely practical viewpoint, there are far more women who will sleep for money with an older man than there are men who will do the same for an older woman.) Similarly, it is morally easier for an older man to accept the idea of an affair, or some other variety of "illicit" relationship.

However, this attitude may be changing. Dr. Paul Glick, senior demographer with the population division of the U.S. Census Bureau, has reported that more than eighteen thousand couples over sixty-five listed themselves in the last census as unmarried and living together. This is surely a vast underestimate of the actual number. Those who deal with older persons—gerontologists, counselors, retirement-community administrators—say that the aged are increasingly pairing off in long-term affairs. For some, it is a purely practical matter, a way to preserve maximum Social Security income and to keep the "widow's benefits" from company or union pensions —payments that are usually cut off if a woman remarries. (It also cuts down interference from children worried about the possibility of losing their inheritance if a parent remarries.) For others, it may be an "unmarriage of convenience," a way of sharing chores, alleviating loneliness. But for a growing number of older couples, living together is seen as a logical solution to their desire for emotional closeness and sexual expression.

They do not take the step easily. Struggling with guilt, many seek guidance from ministers who themselves must struggle to sort out the conflicts among legalities, religious principles, and compassion. For example, the Rev. Dr. Benton Gaskell, minister of the Pilgrim United Church in Pomona, California, whose congregation of more than two thousand people includes a high percentage of over-sixty-fives, told of a couple, both widowed, who came to him for help.

"They were in their seventies," he said, "and living together clandestinely because they couldn't afford to marry since they would lose pension income. They said they felt 'faithless' to their late spouses, never knew what to tell their children or friends, and were in spiritual distress over their predicament. They asked me to ease their guilt by solemnizing their union in the sight of God."

For Dr. Gaskell, the plea presented a quandary. A minister may not conduct a marriage ceremony if there is no marriage license. Nor could he compromise the church. Yet he could not turn away the couple's plea. After consultation with his staff, Dr. Gaskell fashioned a ritual that enabled him formally to bless the couple's "union." With this emotional support, the couple were able to live together openly. "I don't know what they told friends or family," says Dr. Gaskell, "and I don't care. I know what they told me. 'We feel better about ourselves now,' they said. 'It makes us feel our relationship is all right.' "

Are our sexual drives and capacities really so persistent and long-lasting? From time to time, a scientist returns from such Shangri-Las as Hunza, Soviet Georgia, or an Andean village in Ecuador with reports of virile octogenarians. Dr. Alexander Leaf of the Harvard Medical School, who has been to all three of those centers of longevity, recently reported that he was convinced that "a vigorous life—sexual activity included—was possible for at least one hundred years. . . ." Occasionally, too, a charismatic elder offers similar evidence: a Chaplin, a Picasso, a Senator Thurmond fathering children late in life; or Somerset Maugham complaining, in his eighties, that "one loses one's looks and desirability; yet the desire itself remains."

But is that also true for the typical older man or woman? To echo Dr. Calderone, the answer is yes—and much of the sexual indignity the aged suffer could be eased if the biological facts were better known. The three most significant studies of geriatric sexual behavior have been made by Kinsey, Duke's Center for the Study of Aging, and Masters and Johnson. In each, the findings clearly show that men and women in a state of general good health are physiologically able to have a satisfying sex life well into their seventies, eighties, and beyond. The studies also indicate that those who were most active sexually during youth and middle age usually retain their vigor and interest longer into old age.

Though Kinsey interviewed only a small number of older persons, his was the pioneering survey. It showed for the first time that four out of five men over the age of sixty were capable of intercourse, and that there was no evidence of sexual decline in women until much later in life. The Duke studies, which have been conducted on a continuing basis for twenty years, are unique in that researchers have been able to follow the trend of sexuality in aging individuals over a sustained time period. One fascinating result was evidence that 15 percent of men and women studied showed a steady *rising* rate of sexual interest and activity as they got older.

While such a complex survey as Duke's cannot be simplistically summarized, the main findings indicate that two out of three men are sexually active past sixty-five, and one out of five is still active in his eighties. And though activity may decline, interest remains: About half of the eighty- and ninety-year-olds reported a moderate degree of interest. The story is somewhat different for women. "In their sixties," writes Duke's Dr. Eric Pfeiffer, "about one in three reports sexual interest while only one in five is actually having sex. However, their rates of interest and activity don't seem to fall off with increasing age." There are several obvious explanations for the lower activity rate for women: the lack of available men, a greater reluctance to accept nonmarital sex, more anxiety over physical appearance, and a willingness to believe that sex is, or should be, ended after menopause.

Dr. William Masters and Virginia Johnson not only interviewed the aged but also clinically monitored their sexual performance. For one thing, this helped to discount faulty memory, wishful thinking, bragging, or its converse, embarrassed understatement. For another, it provided the first detailed picture of the older body's physiological sexual reactions. Masters and Johnson found that a man's capacity for erection and climax, and a woman's capacity for orgasm, were slowed but not terminated by the aging process. "Inevitably," they say, "all physical responses are slowed. . . . A man can't run around the block as fast as he could twenty or thirty years previously. Yet the simple fact that his sexual functioning is but one more element of his total physiologic functioning may never occur to him.". . .

Every day, four thousand more Americans reach the age of sixty-five, and they can expect an average of fifteen more years of life. What is truly distressing is that those who deal with the rapidly growing number of older persons—family and friends, doctors and social workers, staffs of old-age homes—are either unaware of the data proving the sexual interest and capability of the aged or cannot psychologically accept it. Just as Freud's findings about childhood sexuality met enormous emotional resistance at first, so are the discoveries about sexuality in the aged. Some authorities manage to reject them altogether. For example, a current book, *How to Deal with Aging and the Elderly,* states: "Most persons lose interest somewhere along the line. . . . A normal development is a displacement of passionate physical sexual relations for a deeper marital relationship that revolves more about . . . philosophical thought about the hereafter."

This sort of attitude cuts older persons off from reassuring information, deprives them of helpful guidance, and reinforces their own sense of shame for still having sexual feelings. Dr. Laura Singer-Magdoff, a New York therapist and former president of the American Association of Marriage and Family Counselors, recently included the topic of sexuality in a talk she gave to a group of older persons. "A gray-haired woman about seventy came up to me with tears in her eyes," the counselor recalled. "She said it was the first time anyone had discussed sex in old age as if it were a normal thing."

The men and women in nursing and old-age homes are probably the most deprived on this score. Their environment is almost totally desexualized. It is considered progress when dining or recreation halls and residential wings are not sex-segregated. Privacy is virtually nonexistent: the administrator of one Delaware convalescent home told me that her staff respected patients' privacy, but added that "we run a bed check every two hours to make sure they are all right." Only a minority of institutions make an effort to provide areas where a couple can be alone together even to talk, much less to court. Dr. Calderone cites an instance in which one home forbade any unmarried man and woman to watch television together late in the evening. Even married couples may be separated; some state institutions segregate them, or permit the sexes to mix only under "supervision." If only one spouse is in a home, the other seldom has the right to privacy during a visit. A vigorous woman of seventy-one recently complained to the director of a convalescent home, because there was neither the opportunity nor the facility for her to have a sexual relationship with her husband, who was a patient there. "He entered the home to be cared for during his recovery from a serious eye operation," the woman said. "I can't take care of him properly at home. But there is nothing else wrong with him, no reason why we cannot make love. Yet when I come to visit him, we must meet only in public areas. Even if we *could* be alone in his room, there's only a narrow hospital bed there. When I suggested to the home's director that he put at least a three-quarter bed in my husband's room, the man looked at me as if I were some sort of sexual monster."

"Society tends to say," observes Dr. Calderone, " 'You should be finished with sex—especially since trying to meet your sexual needs adds to the bother of looking after you.' " Thus staff members, from administrators to attendants, for the most part avoid any reference to the idea that their residents may have sexual needs or even feelings. An older person who evidences them in any way is often reproved or considered sick or depraved—the "dirty old man" label again.

In its fifteen years of existence, the American Nursing Home Association, which includes seven thousand public and private facilities, has never scheduled a discussion of sexuality at any of its meetings. A spokeswoman said the American Association of Homes for the Aging was "concerned" about residents' sexual rights—the AAHA is in the process of drawing up a "Patient's Bill of Rights" that includes privacy—but added that the topic was "sort of taboo, people don't like to think about it, and since it isn't a frontline issue, we don't concentrate on it." (In fairness, some distinctions should be drawn. Many homes care for the chronically ill, for whom sex is not an issue. Publicly supported homes operate under legislative restrictions. Some privately supported ones have large budgets and trained staffs, while others are short of money, facilities, and trained personnel. Some reflect conservative community mores or the conventional attitudes of their administrators. And all believe they have to deal with problems far more important than geriatric sexuality.)

Nevertheless, some small progress is being made. According to Hannah Weiner, a sociologist and head of a counseling group called SOMA (Services to Ongoing Mature Aging), this can range from establishing beauty parlors in old-age homes to scheduling talks on sex by gynecologists and urologists. A few homes now set aside small lounges where one or two couples can talk or have tea. Too, SOMA has had an encouraging response from institutions to the "sexuality and aging" seminars it conducts.

But no amount of frills or lectures can substitute for privacy, and certainly not for a more understanding approach. "Those are needed most," says Jacob Reingold, executive director of the modern, six-hundred-guest Hebrew Home for the Aged on the banks of the Hudson in New York City. An energetic and empathic man, Mr. Reingold once shocked a nurse who came running to him to report that an elderly couple were making love in the woman's room. "What should I do?" the nurse asked frantically. Answered Mr. Reingold: "Tiptoe gently out so you don't disturb them."

Recently, a Canadian doctor suggested that all old-age homes should set aside "petting rooms." But privacy is important, Mr. Reingold points out, not so much to isolate affection or intimacy as to give it legitimacy. "Because of their cultural background," he says, "older people tend to separate what's 'right' in public from what's 'right' in private. So a woman rebuffs a man's overtures, or a man turns a blind eye to a little flirting—but I think they would act differently if there weren't so many witnesses. They are caught in a bind. Either they behave 'acceptably' and miss out on emotional satisfactions, or feel they must run the risk of disapproval and embarrassment."

We may be slowly acclimating ourselves to the idea that there is sexuality after sixty-five, but we are still a long way from actively helping older people to express it fully, or to deal with their feelings about it. That is the opinion of Dr. Robert N. Butler, a Washington, D.C. psychiatrist and an expert in the mental health of the aging. *Aging & Mental Health,* which he has written with Myrna I. Lewis, a mental health specialist, calls for "positive psychosocial approaches" to the question. "What we need," the authors say, "is a campaign of sex education for the aged. For example, techniques of intercourse especially pertinent to the needs of older people should be clarified. Thus, sex in the morning may be preferable for those who fatigue easily at night. Certain coital positions may make intercourse more feasible for those who are crippled by arthritis."

Butler feels doctors have a responsibility to be

more specific about the sexual effects of medical problems. A man or woman with a heart condition, for instance, ought to know that a coronary attack during sex occurs much less often than the patient may fear is the case. "If a person is taking nitroglycerine pills as medication," says Butler, "there's no reason he can't take one *before* beginning intercourse, as a precautionary measure to ease his concern. A woman who experiences vaginal discomfort should be encouraged to have hormonal replacement therapy, even in her older years. A man facing a prostatectomy should be reassured that the likelihood of impotence resulting is comparatively small. And if a doctor has a choice among the varying techniques for that surgery, he should consider the sexual effects in making his decision."

Butler also inveighs against the indiscriminate dosing of old people with tranquilizers and antidepressants, often just to make them "easier to handle." One of the pills' side effects is to cut sexual drive and inhibit ejaculation. "The average doctor," says Butler, "does not really think sex matters in old age." For example, a seventy-two-year-old man recently asked his physician's help just before he planned to remarry. During the past two or three years, the man had experienced lessened potency. Occasionally, he could not achieve an erection at all. He wondered if he could be given hormone pills or an injection that would help him. "The woman I'm going to marry is a wonderful person, and I don't want to embarrass or disappoint her," the man said. Instead of examining the man to see if anything could be done medically to aid him, the doctor dismissed the idea as not worth bothering about. "If she's a wonderful woman," he pontificated, "she'll understand."

But sexual activity can actually be therapeutic for

an older person. "There is some evidence," says Butler, "that it helps arthritics by increasing adrenal-gland output of cortisone. The sex act also helps to reduce psychological tension."

But though Butler and other experts believe that much can be done to improve the physical aspects of sex for the aged, they emphasize that, in the best sense, older persons should be encouraged to explore the broader emotional limits of sexuality. Researchers focus on quantitative questions—outlet, frequency, response. They seldom seek answers to qualitative questions—needs, desires, hopes.

"Perhaps I am romanticizing," Butler says, "but old age may be the time to make sex a work of art. It would be tragic if older persons seek merely to recapture the physical sensations of their younger days. Age offers the opportunity to view sex as intimate communication in its best sense."

Clearly, there is more to sexuality after sixty-five than just the act of sex. For a man, there is the satisfaction of feeling still masculine; for a woman, still feminine; for both, still being wanted and needed. There is the comforting warmth of physical nearness, the pleasure of companionship. There is the rewarding emotional intimacy of shared joys. All we need, the song says, is love, love, love. Do not those who are older need it as much as any of us?

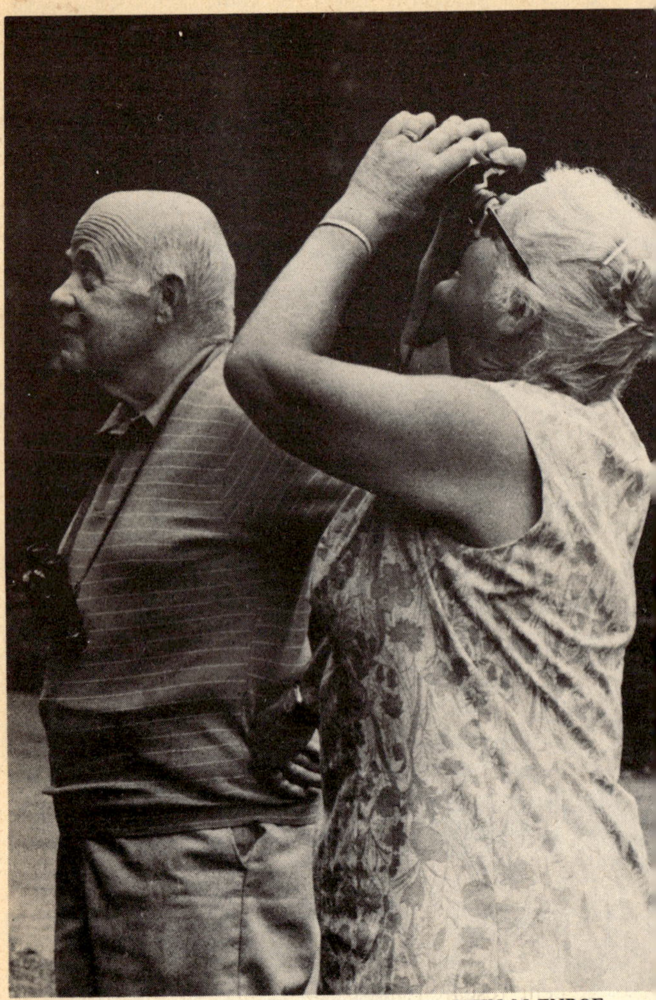

JOHN McENROE

Many older couples like this one find that inexpensive hobbies such as birdwatching can make the later years a fascinating, rewarding, and enjoyable time to be alive.

4

Grow Old Along With Me! The Best Is Yet to Be

by BERNICE L. NEUGARTEN

The following selection by one of our country's most distinguished gerontologists reminds us that not all old people are poor, sick, and lonely. Many are quite happy. She indicates that despite the adjustments that age often necessitates, there are many different ways of adapting. And perhaps most importantly, she warns us that if we wish to avoid ageism and generation gaps, we must avoid stereotyping the old.

MOST OF US have a half-conscious and irrational fear that one day we will find ourselves old, as if suddenly we will fall off a cliff, and that what we *will be* then has little to do with what we *are* now. Recent research has shown, however, that nothing could be farther from the truth.

"Grow Old Along With Me! The Best Is Yet to Be" by Bernice L. Neugarten, from *Psychology Today*, December 1971.

It would be a gross oversimplification, of course, to say that no changes occur in personality as people move from middle age through old age, just as it would be a distortion to say that life-styles always remain consistent. But within broad limits—and with no overwhelming biological accidents—the pattern of aging is predictable for the individual if we know his personality in middle age and how he has dealt with earlier life events.

Several years' research that I and other investigators have done at the University of Chicago has led us to conclude that aging should be seen as one part of the continuous life cycle. It is shaped by the individual's past—his childhood, adolescence, and adulthood. Like earlier periods in life, aging brings new situations and new problems. It calls for new adaptations.

Middle age and old age are eventful periods, and grandparenthood, retirement, widowhood, illness, and the recognition of approaching death can be as dramatic as anything that happens earlier. In adapting to the biological changes that are going on inside and to the social changes that are going on outside, the aging person draws upon what he has been as well as what he is. How else shall we account for the fact that one person copes well, another poorly, with the succession of late-life events?

Nevertheless, most people see aging as alien to the self and tend to deny or repress the associated feelings of distaste and anxiety. We have an irrational fear of aging and, as a result, we maintain a psychological distance between ourselves and older persons.

This irrational fear has its basis in our stereotypical thinking about age groups. Stereotypes about the young, the middle-aged, and the old influence our behavior in subtle ways. They affect our perceptions of appropriate and inappropriate behavior in ourselves and in other persons. They constrain our attitudes and our actions. They make it difficult to improve relationships among persons of various ages.

While the stereotyping of any age group is full of pitfalls, we are just now beginning to realize that stereotypes about aging and the aged create a particularly complex set of problems. In addition to making us fear aging, the stereotypes lead to a divisiveness in society at large that has been called ageism—that is, negative or hostile attitudes between age groups that lead to socially destructive competition. As long as we believe that old persons are poor, isolated, sick, and unhappy (or, to the contrary, powerful, rigid, and reactionary), we find the prospect of old age particularly unattractive. We can then separate ourselves comfortably from older persons and relegate them to inferior status.

Conflict between generations probably is a universal theme in history, but the intensity of the conflict and the focus of the hostility obviously fluctuate according to historical, social, and economic factors. Some social scientists are alarmed that generational conflicts are increasing in the 1970s. Although the generation gap has been described mainly as a gap between the young and everybody else, it is entirely possible that conflicts will also appear in the other direction—that is, between the old and everybody else.

Anger toward the old may be on the rise. One of every ten Americans is now sixty-five or older, and an industrialized society whose citizens live increasingly longer becomes in many ways a gerontocratic society. Older persons occupy an increasing proportion of power positions in judicial, legislative, economic, and professional areas, and the young and the middle-aged often resent them. Older persons themselves are learning the politics of confrontation. The appeal to Senior Power and the recent growth of national organizations that act as advocates for older persons suggest that the conflict is being joined by those who might otherwise be its victims.

Stereotypes of the aged are difficult to dispel, largely because research on aging is a recent development in both the biological and the social sciences, and research findings reach the public at a snail's pace. Many widely held but inaccurate images, inadvertently repeated through the mass media, come from social workers who serve the poor, the lonely, and the isolated, and from physicians and psychiatrists who see the physically ill and the mentally ill. Thus, we base many of our current stereotypes on a picture of the needy rather than on a picture of the typical older person.

Studies of large and representative samples of older persons are now appearing, however, and they go far toward exploding some of our outmoded images. For example, old persons do not become isolated and neglected by their families, although both generations prefer separate households. Old persons are not dumped into mental hospitals by cruel or indifferent children. They are not necessarily lonely or desolate if they live alone. Few of them ever show overt signs of mental deterioration or senility, and only a small proportion ever become mentally ill. For those who do, psychological and psychiatric treatment is by no means futile.

Retirement and widowhood do not lead to mental illness, nor does social isolation. Retirement is not necessarily bad: some men and women want to keep on working, but more and more choose to retire earlier and earlier. Increasing proportions of the population evidently value leisure more than they value work. Nor do retired persons sicken physically from idleness and feelings of worthlessness. Three-fourths of the persons questioned in a recent national sample reported that they were satisfied or very satisfied with their lives since retirement. This is in line with earlier surveys. Most persons over sixty-five think of themselves as being in good health, and they act accordingly, no matter what their physicians think.

The belief that sixty-five is a useful marker of old age is another stereotype. It was historical accident that set sixty-five as the age of eligibility for Social Security payments. The decision reflected the economic situation and the manpower needs of the country in the 1930s. Age sixty-five otherwise has no reality as a turning point in the life of the individual. Because people are beginning to retire at earlier ages, perhaps we should call sixty or fifty-five the beginning of old age. Or, on the other hand, because sixty-five-year-olds are generally more youthful today than their fathers were and because longevity is increasing, perhaps we should use seventy-five as the marker. (The 1970 U.S. census shows that in the last ten years the number of persons aged seventy-five and over increased three times as fast as the number of those aged sixty-five to seventy-four.)

But the most insidious stereotype of all, in many ways, puts the old (or, for that matter, the young or the middle-aged) into a distinct category or a distinct group. There is, in truth, no such thing as "the" young, or "the" old. People *do* differ; they also become increasingly different over time, as each person accumulates an idiosyncratic set of experiences and becomes committed to a unique set of people, things, interests, and activities. One has only to recall, for instance, the range of differences among the members of one's high-school graduating class and then to see these persons at a class reunion twenty-five years later. They are much more varied as forty-year-olds than they were as eighteen-year-olds. In a society as complex as ours, with increasing social permissiveness for people to follow their own bents, a good case can be made that—despite the counterpressures that create conformity—increased differentiation occurs over the life cycle.

To put the same point another way, calendar age or chronological age is a poor basis for grouping people who have attained biological maturity. Study after study of the happiness, intelligence, personality, or health of adults has shown that age is a poor index of the differences between people.

Older persons are not a homogeneous group, then, no matter from what perspective we look at them. This fact has become particularly clear to our group at Chicago in carrying out a long line of studies of middle age and aging over the past fifteen years: studies of personality, of adaptational patterns, of career lines, of age-norms, of attitudes and values across social-class and generational lines. The number of men and women who have participated now totals more than two thousand. We based each study in the series upon a relatively large sample of normal persons; none was a volunteer, and all were living in one or another metropolitan community in the Midwest.

One study that illustrates the point about heterogeneity focused on persons aged seventy to seventy-nine. We were pursuing these questions: Would retired persons who stayed actively engaged in various family and community activities be happier than those who were relatively inactive? How would longstanding personality differences affect these relationships? To find out, we gathered various psychological test data and conducted home interviews repeatedly over a seven-year period. We made systematic assessments in three areas: personality, degree of satisfaction with life, and extent of social-role activity.

In the area of personality, we assessed each person on forty-five dimensions. Then, by appropriate statistical methods, we derived four major personality types, which we called *integrated, defended, passive-dependent,* and *disintegrated.* . . .

INTEGRATED. The majority of seventy-year-olds remained integrated personalities—well-functioning persons with complex inner lives, intact cognitive abilities and competent egos. They accepted and maintained a comfortable degree of control over their impulses, they were flexible and open to new stimuli, mellow and mature. All were high in life satisfaction. At the same time, they differed among themselves with regard to role activity and therefore showed different patterns of aging.

One pattern we called the *reorganizers,* competent people who were engaged in a wide variety of activities. They were the optimum agers in some respects—at least in the American culture, which places a high value on continuing to be active. These persons substituted new activities for lost ones; when they retired from work, they gave time to community affairs or to the church or to other associations. They reorganized their patterns of activity. One such person was a retired schoolteacher who, at seventy-five, was selling life insurance and making more money than ever. He held elective office in an association of retirees, attended concerts and the theater with his wife, and visited regularly with friends.

Another group of complex and well-integrated personalities we called the *focused,* because they had become selective in their activities, devoting energy to the few roles that were important to them. One was an emeritus university professor who, at seventy-five, was still teaching, but only those courses she wanted to teach. She had withdrawn from organizations that she felt were needlessly time-consuming; she felt free to accept or decline invitations at will. It was a relief to have her husband at home now, because he did things around the house that she had had to do earlier, but otherwise, he played a very secondary role in her life. She seldom saw her children and liked it that way. She was glad to be free of responsibility, and to invest all her energies in her work.

A third pattern we called the *disengaged.* These were also well-integrated personalities with high life satisfaction, but with low activity; they had moved away voluntarily from role commitments, not in response to external losses or physical deficits, but because of preference. These were self-directed, though not shallow, persons. They were interested in the world, but they were not imbedded in networks of social interaction. They had high feelings of self-regard, just as the first two groups did, but they had chosen the "rocking-chair" approach to old age—a calm, withdrawn, but contented pattern. One was a retired man who had dropped his club memberships, seldom saw his former work colleagues or friends, and welcomed the opportunity to lead a relaxed life at home, visiting with his children and grandchildren, gardening a little, and occasionally helping his wife around the house.

DEFENDED. In the next major personality category were men and women whom we called "armored" or "defended." These were the striving, ambitious, and achievement-oriented persons who drove themselves hard. They had high defenses against anxiety and needed to maintain tight control over impulse life. This personality group provided two patterns of aging.

The *holding-on* pattern included the persons who said, "As long as you keep busy, you'll get along all right," or "I'll work until I drop." This group had medium to high life satisfaction because they managed to maintain relatively high levels of activity. One such woman had been an office worker all her life, had never married, and regarded herself as strong and tough. She said that when she was younger she was much too busy to feel lonely; now that she was retired, she kept busy as the historian and recording secretary for the local DAR. She had arteriosclerosis and had suffered a heart attack five years earlier, but she said that she did not let her illness get her down: "You can't slow down just because you happen to have some physical limitations."

The other group of defended personalities we called the *constricted*. These persons were busy defending themselves against aging; preoccupied with losses and deficits, they constricted their social interactions and shut out new experiences, fending off what they seemed to regard as imminent collapse. Given their personalities, their approach to the world worked fairly well, and they had medium or even high levels of satisfaction and contentment. Mr. B., for example, had worked out elaborate rituals for maintaining his health. He talked of little else. He and his wife spent hours shopping for just the right foods, and they made vegetable juices fresh every day. He took long drives into the country each week to bring back pure spring water. He was not much different now, he said, from when he was younger. All his life he had been cautious about himself, and even as a young man he "always thought twice before making any rash decisions."

PASSIVE-DEPENDENT. Among members of the passive-dependent group, there were also two patterns of aging.

The *succorance-seeking* were those persons with strong dependency needs who sought responsiveness from others. They showed medium levels of activity, for the most part, and medium satisfaction with life; they did fairly well as long as each had at least one or two other persons to lean on. One woman, for example, looked back to the time when her husband was alive, because he always took such good care of her. Now she was diabetic and felt particularly helpless. But she said she counted on her son, who lived in the same city and visited her every day. He took her shopping on Saturdays, paid all her bills, and saw to it that she took her medicine.

There were a small number of the *apathetic,* those in whom passivity was the most striking personality feature. They had few activities and very little interaction with others; they showed little interest in the world about them. Life was hard, they said, and there was never much that could be done about it, was there? One, for instance, was a woman who limited her activities entirely to meeting her physical needs and caring for her two cats. She seldom interacted even with her brother and sister-in-law, who lived on the floor above her, because, as she said, "They are old and sick, too, and don't go anywhere."

DISINTEGRATED. Finally, there were a few whom we called the distintegrated or *disorganized,* persons who showed gross defects in psychological functions and deterioration in thought processes. They managed to maintain themselves in the community, either because of protective families or because of the forbearance of the people around them. Mr. G., for instance, was a paranoid, isolated man who lived in a run-down section of the city. He did a little janitorial work around the building in exchange for a room in the basement.

These eight patterns do not exhaust the variations we found in this group of seventy-year-olds, and the group itself did not include the full range. There are, of course, some persons in their seventies who are too ill to be interviewed, a small number who live in hospitals and homes for the aged, and a few who have moved to leisure communities in the South and Southwest.

But it is the variation rather than the similarity among seventy-year-olds that is impressive. And the diversity is likely to become even greater in the future. At present, there is an overrepresentation of the foreign-born, the poorly educated, and the poor among those who are sixty-five and over. In future decades, with better health, more education, and more financial resources, older men and women will have greater freedom to choose life-styles that suit them.

Another point is equally important. The individuals we studied in such great detail over seven years seemed to show relatively consistent patterns of coping and adjustment. Although we had no systematic data gathered when these persons were young or middle-aged, we knew a great deal about their life histories, and we had information from family members. The general picture was one of personality continuities over time.

Looked at realistically, then, and with the stereotypes dispelled, aging is not a leveler of individual differences. For most people, it brings no sudden and drastic transformation of personality. This being so, aging will not separate the individual's present from his future self. Just as every person changes as he grows up, he will continue to change as he grows old. But aging will not destroy the continuities between what he has been, what he is, and what he will be. Recognition of this fact should lessen the fear of growing old. At the social level, the knowledge that our stereotypes are ill-founded should make older persons seem less distant and less alien, and should help to bridge the psychological barriers between people of different ages.

The Manager

by JOHN O'HARA

5

Fiction can often give us a more accurate **feeling** for a situation than a non-fiction piece of writing can. In this selection, we can almost experience the indignities suffered by the elderly Mr. Wilbur and his friends. Because less money can be made from them, because some of them have health problems, and because sex is considered "undignified" for them, a manager of a lodge and the society he represents discriminate, often in subtle ways, against them.

THE WILBURS always arrived at the Inn a little before or a little after the summer season. True, in recent years, with the popularity of skiing, the Inn enjoyed two seasons, but a very different sort patronized the place when the snow was on the ground. The Wilburs were quite definitely not of the skiing crowd.

Gray Hair Changes Gradually To Young Natural Look

If the years have stolen the natural color and oils from your hair, leaving it gray, streaked, dry, drab, faded, or mousey; simply use Herbold Pomade as your hair dressing. It will blend in lasting color just right for your hair, but will not change its shade; only brighten it.

As grayness gradually disappears your hair becomes lustrous, lively, easy to control, and young looking again.

If you want to, you may leave some gray showing, or keep sideburns gray.

Your improved younger look is so real, so subtle, so gradual, no one notices you are using anything but a fine hair dressing.

Not a coal tar dye, but a special hair cream, that keeps the gray away by replacing lost color and oils, so vital to young, healthy looking well-groomed hair. Start using Herbold Pomade now, as your exclusive hair dressing to keep from looking old and gray. For Men and Women at Drug and Cosmetic Counters.

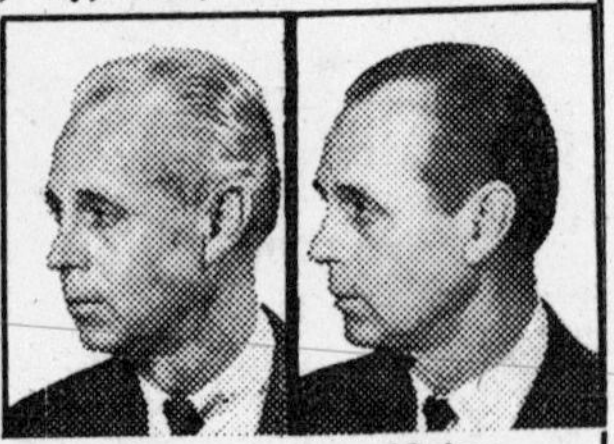

Before 10 days

Herbold Pomade

CREAM $1.25 & $3, LIQUID $2

Use Creamy Pomade to condition dry hair. Liquid Pomade for normal hair. Both tone down gray hair.

HERBOLD LABORATORY, INC.

This advertisement is a good example of the way in which society stresses the importance of looking young. The overall effect of such advertising has been to isolate and exclude older people from the mainstream of American society.

There had been a time when the Wilburs were summer regulars, with their same room and their same table year after year, and paying the summer rates. But after thirty seasons they came only in the spring and the fall, when reduced rates were in effect, and these visits were shorter. "We don't like to let a year go by without a week or so at the Inn," said Mrs. Wilbur. "But now you have to charge almost as much for a single day as we used to pay for a week. Oh, we understand why. But it *is* a shame, isn't it?"

"It is indeed," said Mr. Greene, the proprietor. "We've lost some of our summer people on account of it. But there always seem to be others to take their places."

"Where do you suppose they get the money?" said Mrs. Wilbur. "I know that's a foolish question, but these younger people. I mean the ones in their forties. They can't possibly get away with deducting the cost as a business expense."

"Well, naturally I don't inquire into where they get it, as long as they do. But they seem to have it. Your room goes for twelve hundred for the month of August. A thousand for the month of July. And next year I don't know what it'll be. Won't be any less, that's for sure." Once, and only once, Mr. Greene had had to tell Mrs. Wilbur that much as he would like to give old patrons a special rate, the fact was that he could not make an exception for anyone. Not anyone. Not Colonel and Mrs. Broadbill. Not the Reverend and Mrs. George W. T. Magee. Not Miss Polly Woodward, whose father and mother had been the second couple to sign the registry in 1894. Mrs. Wilbur—and Mr. Greene knew it—was not so much advocating a special rate for the Broadbills and the Magees and Polly Woodward as trying

"Sorry, madam! . . . It's a firm Mother Jones policy not to accept applicants over 35! . . ."

"GRIN AND BEAR IT" BY GEORGE LICHTY—COURTESY OF PUBLISHERS HALL SYNDICATE

A well-known cartoonist takes a satirical look at ageism in hiring practices.

to learn whether they got one. Mr. Greene was too polite to say it, but the stern fact was that even at the full rate the Inn was not making much money off the Broadbills and those others. They spent no money in the Colonial Taproom. Colonel and Mrs. Broadbill had their nip of bourbon before coming down to dinner; the others did not drink at all. And it was not only a question of the money they did not spend; there was their appearance, which was noticeably inhibiting on the younger guests, those couples in their forties who had cocktails before every meal and liqueurs in the Taproom every evening after dinner. As for the Wilburs, Mr. Wilbur was afflicted with some liver ailment that made him appear to be sunburnt in patches on his forehead and cheeks. Young children stared at him, and several young wives had asked to have their table changed so that they would not have to look at him. He was a perfectly nice man, a gentleman, well dressed and neatly groomed; but as one young woman said, very unappetizing. One child of ten had asked him, "Were you *burned?*" and Mr. Wilbur had replied, "In a manner of speaking, yes." The child's mother was infuriated, embarrassed by her daughter's forwardness, but far more annoyed that someone like Mr. Wilbur was there to provoke the child's rude curiosity. Mr. Greene heard all about that. He did nothing, since there was nothing he could do; but he was greatly relieved when the Wilburs advised him that the next year, 1959, they would not be needing their old room in August. They were going to be traveling—they did not say where—and hoped they would be able to stop at the Inn for a week or so in late September. Mr. Greene in his reply expressed regret untinged with sorrow, and advised the Wilburs that he would be unable to guarantee their getting their old room back in 1960 if they relinquished it in '59. Another couple—perhaps the Wilburs remembered them, the Lamports, from Toledo, Ohio—had applied for the Wilburs' room for '59 and subsequent years and Mr. Greene, or the Inn, was redecorating to suit Mrs. Lamport. He was sure the Wilburs would understand. They did.

But they kept coming back. In '59 they stayed two weeks in the latter half of September; in '60, a week in May; in '61, they came for the first week in October. Mr. Greene was not unhappy to see them go. He liked Mr. Wilbur, but he hoped the Wilburs would never come back, because on the Sunday evening during dinner, with the dining room and the Taproom filled almost to capacity, Mr. Wilbur suddenly rose, with a napkin to his mouth, and hurried out of the dining room, fighting back a vomiting spell and barely making the men's room in the lobby.

Mr. Greene, from his position behind the main desk, saw it all happen. It was distressing to see the immediate effect on the men and women in the dining room—and not many had failed to see Mr. Wilbur, with the napkin at his mouth, staggering out toward the lobby. Nevertheless Mr. Greene obeyed the impulse to follow Mr. Wilbur, and in the men's room he found Mr. Wilbur lying on the floor, hemorrhaging from the mouth. Mr. Wilbur looked up at Mr. Greene with the eyes of a dog pleading not to be shot, then fainted away. Two young doctors, who were dining with their wives, entered the men's room. "Get him to a hospital," said one doctor. "I'll stay with him till the ambulance comes." There was nothing more Mr. Greene could do after sending for the ambulance, and he went looking for Mrs. Wilbur. In time he found her, sitting in the lobby with Colonel and Mrs. Broadbill.

"Oh, Mr. Greene, I didn't think it was right to go into the men's room. How is he?"

"There are two doctors in there with him, I guess they're doing all they can till the ambulance gets here."

"The hospital? Did they say he had to go to the hospital?"

"Now don't you worry, Edwina," said Colonel Broadbill. "I had the same thing happen to me six years ago."

"They'll want to give him transfusions, most likely," said Mrs. Broadbill. "They did with Clement."

"They sure did," said Colonel Broadbill. "Whole bunch of fellows from the Army and Navy Club volunteered, but there weren't but two had my type of blood. Mike—"

"Do you think I ought to go in there now, I mean the men's room?" said Mrs. Wilbur.

"Oh, that part'll be all right, Mrs. Wilbur. Yes, I'd go in if I were you," said Mr. Greene.

"Good Lord, Edwina, you don't have to stand on ceremony at a time like this," said the colonel. "You go right in there and pay no attention."

"Would you like me to go with you?" said Mrs. Broadbill. "Goodness me, the places I've been. I'll go in with you."

"I'd appreciate it if you would, Lillian."

"Mr. Greene and I will look out for everything," said the colonel.

Mr. Greene did not quite know what the colonel had in mind, but he was already uncomprehending of Mrs. Wilbur's ability to sit in the lobby while her husband could be bleeding to death a few feet away, behind a door marked Gentlemen.

"Hit him all of a sudden," said Colonel Broadbill. "We just finished our dinner and I was here having my cigar. Mizz Broadbill won't let me smoke one of these Castro cigars in the bedroom, she calls them. Ever since Castro, we haven't been able to get any good Havana leaf, and I must say I go along with Mizz Broadbill. But I do like a cigar after dinner, good or bad. Mrs. Wilbur said he ate too much of the paté. He ate his and then he ate hers, and it was just too rich for him. You set too good a table, Mr. Greene. That hard sauce you give us with the Brown Betty, I have to order seconds on it every time. Now that I don't have to worry about my teeth anymore, I eat those things like your hard sauce as if I were a schoolboy. Sweets. I eat too many sweets."

Mr. Greene wanted to get in a denial that the liver paté had had anything to do with Mr. Wilbur's attack, but the colonel had raised so many points that called for denials that Mr. Greene ignored them all. "How long did they keep you in the hospital, Colonel?" he said.

"How long did they keep me in the hospital?"

"Roughly. Approximately," said Mr. Greene.

"Roughly a week."

"I suppose that means they'll keep Mr. Wilbur that long," said Mr. Greene.

As it turned out, he was wrong. By the time the ambulance arrived Mr. Wilbur was up on his feet, and he stubbornly—for him, angrily—refused to leave the Inn. The doctors said they would not be responsible; Mr. Wilbur said he would absolve them of any responsibility. The ambulance driver said there would still be a charge of thirty dollars, and Mr. Greene paid that and said he would put it on Mr. Wilbur's bill.

Mr. Greene saw the Wilburs off in the morning. They had a well-kept Dodge station wagon, six or seven years old. Mrs. Wilbur was doing the driving, as she always did nowadays, but they had a long ride ahead and Mr. Greene, taking a good look at Mr. Wilbur, was convinced he would never see him again. Mr. Wilbur was all bundled up in his old polo coat and a thick woolen scarf, and a robe over his legs; the brim of his hat turned down all around, and a large area of his face hidden by his sunglasses. He was a pitiful sight. Mrs. Wilbur, however, sitting back confidently, with her hands resting on the steering wheel, seemed capable of driving the car as far as San Francisco.

"I'd rest easier if you phoned me when you get home," said Mr. Greene. "Reverse the charges, of course."

"Oh, now, Mr. Greene, that's very nice of you, but I'm all right. We'll be home before dark," said Mr. Wilbur.

"Not before dark, Lewis, but not long after," said Mrs. Wilbur. "It gets dark earlier now."

They lived in a place called Uniontown, Pennsylvania, and that evening, while he was having his dinner, Mr. Greene was called to the telephone. The Wilburs had had a pleasant trip, stopping for lunch at a very nice motel near Scranton, PA. Mr. Wilbur had not eaten very much for lunch; milk toast, as a matter of fact. Then they had stopped again for a cup of tea at a Howard Johnson on the Pennsylvania Turnpike. A cup of tea with lemon and a little nibble of toast was as much as he wanted. He was in bed now, and the family doctor was coming in to see him later in the evening. Mr. Wilbur had insisted on her making the call, and he wanted to thank Mr. Greene for taking an interest, and to tell him how sorry he was to have caused such a disturbance the night before. He was still weak, naturally, and Mrs. Wilbur had put him right to bed when they got home; but there was nothing to worry about. She had not even bothered to telephone their daughter, who lived in Pittsburgh, but Mr. Wilbur had insisted on her telephoning Mr. Greene. They hoped to be back in the spring, and Mr. Greene said he hoped they would be back. Mrs. Wilbur said she thought their three minutes was up, so she rung off.

Now and then, through the winter months, Mr. Greene would give a thought to the Wilburs, not of the Wilburs independently but as typical of the older crowd, who hung on and hung on in spite of the high rates (which did not affect them all), and the younger summer crowd and their children, who were now the favorite guests of the Inn. If the Wilburs and the Broadbills, people like that, ever had a good look at the skiing crowd, sitting on the floor in their stretch pants, they would not recognize the place. And Mr. Greene wished the old-timers could have a look at the ski crowd; it would tell the old-timers most effectively that the Inn was going along with the times. It would remind them that they had always been given good value at the Inn (and why else would they have come back year after year?); that he had worked hard to make them comfortable; that their steady patronage did not really entitle them to any special rights—or rates.

Mr. Greene liked the new young faces and figures of the ski crowd. They were such a welcome relief from the Wilburs and the Broadbills and the Polly Woodwards. The older ones would come back to the Inn, having been absent eight or ten months, which was just long enough for the passage of time to make those depressing changes in their countenances and in their figures and their gait. Miss Polly Woodward was almost blind, and only in 1962 had she at last begun to carry a cane. Colonel Broadbill had a breath that would knock you over, and it was not from alcohol. Mrs. Broadbill's stockings were always falling down, and when they were not falling down they clung so loosely to her skinny legs that they looked like long underwear. He could not complain about Mrs. Wilbur's appearance; too many of the other guests had been saying for years that *there* was a handsome woman, a woman who aged gracefully. But he had never liked Mrs. Wilbur. Let something, anything, go wrong, and Mrs. Wilbur noticed it, whether it was a malfunction of the plumbing or an erroneous item on the bill. And who else would have complained that the liver paté was so rich that it had made her husband sick? Mr. Greene hoped that he would never have to see Mrs. Wilbur again.

His wish was gratified.

One afternoon in May he was standing in the driveway, having a look at the newly painted shutters on the upper stories, when a station wagon drew up slowly. It came to a stop directly behind him, and as he was not expecting any arrivals that day, and as it was an expensive English car, he assumed it was bringing some drop-in trade for the Taproom.

"Hello there, Mr. Greene!"

Mr. Greene had a better look, and now he saw Mr. Wilbur on the front seat, but the woman at the wheel was not Mrs. Wilbur. "Why, it's Mr. Wilbur. This is a nice surprise."

Mr. Wilbur, in his same old polo coat but wearing a tweed cap that had a little strap in the back, got out of the car and shook hands with Mr. Greene.

He looked extremely well for a man who had gone through so many ailments. "I don't see Mrs. Wilbur," said Mr. Greene.

"No, I'm afraid Mrs. Wilbur passed away during the winter. Heart. We'd never known anything about it. At least she'd never mentioned it to me. Halfway up the stairs one morning, she collapsed, and that was the end."

"I'm very sorry to hear that," said Mr. Greene. "But you're looking well."

"Well, thank you. I had quite a siege myself. They took out over half of my stomach. I was just beginning to get around a bit when Mrs. Wilbur had her attack. The young lady with me is my nurse. Do you suppose you could put us up, two nice single rooms not too far apart?"

"Why yes. I can give you adjoining. Twelve and Fourteen are vacant. You know them, there on the east side where you get the morning sun."

The nurse had parked the car and now joined them. "Miss Buckley, this is Mr. Greene, our famous host. Mr. Greene, my nurse, Miss Buckley."

"I'm very pleased to meet you. Mr. Wilbur speaks very highly of you."

"Pleased to meet you," said Mr. Greene. "Mr. Wilbur's one of our most valued guests. Has been for a good many years."

"Well, the Inn has always been one of my favorite institutions in *my* life. And thanks largely to Mr. Greene, I might add."

"How long will you be with us, you and Miss Buckley?" said Mr. Greene.

"Till Monday at least, maybe a few days longer if you still have room for us."

"I may have to move you out of Twelve and Fourteen, but we'll find something."

"Miss Buckley doesn't mind sharing a bathroom with me," said Mr. Wilbur. "So if you have rooms with an adjoining bath, that'd be all right. I've been a patient of hers for so long now."

"Aaw, now, don't make it sound too long," said Miss Buckley. "He'll think you want to get rid of me."

"Now you know better than that, Miss Buckley," said Mr. Wilbur. "Well, shall we go in and register?"

"I'll send Chester out for your luggage," said Mr. Greene.

"Oh, I'm glad you still have Chester," said Mr. Wilbur. "He's in his sixties, but strong as an ox."

"Age doesn't make that much difference," said Miss Buckley. "If a man takes proper care of himself."

"That doesn't account for Chester. I have to fire him every so often, when he gets to thinking he owns what's in the cellar."

"Well, maybe if he didn't do that he'd get all tensed up," said Miss Buckley. "This man has three ounces of bourbon every night preceding dinner, and I see that he gets it. The best thing in the world for him."

"I'd miss it, no doubt about it," said Mr. Wilbur. "I'm getting to be a drinker in my old age."

"*Stop* with that talk about old age," said Miss Buckley. "I almost wasn't going to let him come here when he started talking about the good times he had here. You'd think he wanted to come here to be buried."

"That was at first. I haven't been talking that way lately, have I?"

"No, I'll admit that, or I wouldn't have let you come," said Miss Buckley.

"Mr. Greene remembers one unfortunate episode."

"Oh, think nothing of it, Mr. Wilbur."

. . . Mr. Greene knew perfectly well what went on among the ski crowd. It would have taken an army of Pinkertons to do an hourly bed check, and as long as order was maintained in the Taproom and the bedrooms were not occupied by more guests than were on the registry, Mr. Greene was not going to try to be everywhere at once. They were young, healthy, vigorous people, with large appetites in every sense of the word. To try to police their behavior would be like going against nature and the times. But if he was willing to overlook certain things with the ski crowd, he had never relaxed his vigilance where the summer people were concerned. Through the years the Inn had acquired a reputation for respectability that was second to none. (Some of the ski crowd had told Mr. Greene that they had heard about that respectability from their parents and grandparents, and that because of it the younger ones were felt to be in safe hands.) A newcomer to the Inn was always asked who had recommended the place, and a letter would go off to the referred-to party so that the referents would be made to feel some sense of responsibility for the newcomer. Mr. Greene had never tolerated any funny business, no matter what or who. A British lord once showed up with a young American woman who obviously was not his lady, and when Mr. Greene saw the young woman, he looked the Englishman straight in the eye and told him that there had been some mixup in his reservations and that he was afraid he could not accommodate them. He suggested they try a hotel in a city fifty miles away. His lordship knew better than to risk a scene, and out he went, followed by the young woman and Chester with their luggage. In a sense, they were also followed—by a sharp letter from Mr. Greene to the travel agency employed by the Englishman.

The principal stockholders of the Inn, a well-to-do group of men in the insurance business in Hartford, and women, widows, who lived in the Hartford-Springfield area, had complete confidence in Mr. Greene's discretion, integrity, and acumen, and gave him what amounted to carte-blanche. They, too, were well aware of the greater freedom accorded the ski crowd, but they relied on Mr. Greene to keep it well in hand. . . .

It was not so much that Mr. Wilbur was a problem. Mr. Wilbur had been coming to the Inn too long not to be thoroughly indoctrinated in the policies maintained by Mr. Greene. And Mr. Wilbur was not a young man. Mr. Wilbur was an *old* man. But during the few minutes in the driveway Mr. Greene had formed an impression of Miss Buckley that was decidedly not in her favor. The late Mrs. Wilbur, whatever else she was, was a lady, and that much could not be said for Miss Buckley. Mr. Greene resented personally her saying "this man" has three ounces of bourbon, or whatever it was; he resented her saying that *she* was almost not going to let Mr. Wilbur come here. No doubt Mr. Wilbur had been so completely dominated by Mrs. Wilbur that her passing gave him a sense of relief; he certainly had not looked so well, so relaxed, in many years. But Mr. Greene wanted better things for Mr. Wilbur; most of all he wanted Mr. Wilbur to live out his remaining years without loss of the dignity that was perhaps his outstanding characteristic, that indeed had made the episode of the hemorrhage so distressing for Mr. Wilbur and all those who admired him. To be referred to to his face as "this man" was an affront to Mr. Wilbur's dignity, even though *he* might not yet regard it as such.

Mr. Wilbur was not a problem, and yet he was a problem for Mr. Greene. Mr. Greene usually designated as problems the men who got noisy-drunk in the Taproom, guests who antagonized the help, women who had dogs or cats. Mr. Wilbur, by appearing with this Miss Buckley, became a problem for Mr. Greene that was of a different nature from any he had dealt with as manager of the Inn. Mr. Wilbur was a good fifteen—well, a good ten—years older than Mr. Greene, and he needed protection. It came down simply to that: Mr. Wilbur needed protection.

There was a daughter living in Pittsburgh, but Mr. Greene remembered her only as a child and a young girl who was a bit of a scamp. She was not an evil girl, but she had started smoking in the lobby at a too-early age, and several of the older women had spoken to Mr. Greene about the shorts she wore. The Wilburs' daughter had never appeared at the Inn after her marriage, and that was twenty years ago. In any event from what he knew of her she was not likely to concern herself much with her father's undeniable willingness to submit to a Miss Buckley, and Mr. Greene was unhappy. Long ago, as a bellhop and assistant manager, he had learned that old men and old women did not automatically become sexless when youth was gone. He had seen things that were hard to believe, but he had seen them: old women murderously jealous over an old man; lovemaking that belied all the jokes about age and impotence. Twice as a very young man with curly hair and the face of an acolyte he had been propositioned by older people, one of them not a woman. A bellhop of his acquaintance had wheedled a Packard roadster out of one old woman, and was contemptuous of the young Greene for passing up equal opportunities. Dignity therefore meant more than a dignified manner to Mr. Greene; dignity of the right kind was often the only protection the old people had. Lose your dignity, and you are putty in the hands of a Miss Buckley.

Mr. Greene was too fond of Mr. Wilbur to assign to one of the help the task of watching out for any funny business with the nurse. Saying nothing to anyone, he took on the job himself. With his reputation for attention to small details he was more or less expected to pop up here, there, and everywhere in the hotel and on the grounds, a fact that made it easier to keep an eye on Mr. Wilbur and the nurse. Rooms Twelve and Fourteen, though adjoining, were separated by a locked door, and on the morning after Mr. Wilbur's arrival Mr. Greene satisfied himself that both beds had been slept in, and not merely rumpled for show. Throughout the second day, Mr. Greene kept tabs on Mr. Wilbur and the nurse. Mr. Wilbur apparently had a routine; a walk after breakfast; a nap after lunch; a game of gin rummy with Miss Buckley, followed by a perfectly legitimate massage for which Miss Buckley had requested a table. Mr. Wilbur then had his bath, dressed, and came down to the Taproom for his three ounces of bourbon before dinner. In the evening they played gin rummy again, watched the eleven o'clock news on the television set in the lobby, and went up to their rooms. In the course of the day Mr. Greene had spoken to them three or four times, not at any great length but in his offhand, casual, managerial way. Mr. Wilbur made some favorable comments on the dogwood. Miss Buckley admired the abundance of brass trinkets and wondered how they were kept so bright and shiny in these days of irresponsible help. Even in her own profession, the nurses they turned out these days. . . .

Mr. Wilbur and the nurse said goodnight to Mr. Greene as they made their way to the elevator. Mr. Greene had never called a man's face beautiful, but there was a serenity in Mr. Wilbur's half-realized smile that was close to beautiful, and that in spite of the lines and discolorations. Mr. Greene mentally absolved Mr. Wilbur of all wrongdoing, and was chiding himself for suspiciousness. But just as the elevator door was closing Mr. Greene heard Mr. Wilbur laugh in a way that was different from any laugh that had ever come out of Mr. Wilbur. It had almost a cackle to it, that laugh, and Mr. Greene wondered what Miss Buckley had said to provoke it. In an instant Mr. Greene's suspicions all returned. Indeed, the laugh practically confirmed his suspicions of Miss Buckley as a woman who practiced some seductive power over Mr. Wilbur. The elevator was a self-service one, and in Mr. Greene's imagination Miss Buckley had said something to the old man that she would not have said in front of anyone else. The cackling laugh was so horrible that it provided a test of Mr. Greene's fondness for Mr. Wilbur.

The Taproom closed at midnight, and in the more than half-empty Inn all was quiet by a quarter past twelve. Mr. Greene made his final rounds of the Taproom, the lobby, and the other rooms on the main floor. Walter Downs, the night watchman, was on his patrol. No one else was to be seen. Ordinarily it would have been the time of day Mr. Greene liked best, when his work was finished and his guests all safe for the night. But now his job was not enjoyable and his immediate task was unpleasant, as unpleasant as the inferences he had drawn from that laugh of

Mr. Wilbur's. He was certain now that Mr. Wilbur, under the influence of Miss Buckley, had turned into a nasty old man.

"Everything in order, Walter?" said Mr. Greene.

"Everything," said Walter Downs.

"You might have a look around out back, make sure the painter didn't leave any ladders lying around," said Mr. Greene.

"I will. I'll do that after I eat my lunch," said Walter.

"No hurry," said Mr. Greene. He wanted to make sure that Walter would be out of the way for a while. "They're forgetful sometimes. They leave those ladders any place. Person could stumble on them in the dark and we'd have a lawsuit."

"Want me to do it now?"

"No, you go eat your lunch and then do it," said Mr. Greene. "I'll say goodnight to you."

"Goodnight," said Walter Downs, heading for the kitchen.

Mr. Greene took the elevator to the third floor, got out, and walked down to the second floor. It was possible to hear the elevator from Twelve and Fourteen, to judge where it was stopping. He walked down the hall past Twelve and Fourteen, the sound of his steps deadened by the carpeting. The light was on in Fourteen, Miss Buckley's room. It showed in the transom. Twelve was dark. He listened outside Fourteen; Miss Buckley had the radio going softly. Mr. Greene decided that if there was any funny business between Mr. Wilbur and Miss Buckley, it had already been finished for the night. He was somewhat relieved, although he was only postponing the moment when he would catch them together.

He now walked to the end of the hall and pushed the button for the elevator. He heard the machinery go into operation and was waiting for the elevator's slow descent when Miss Buckley's door was opened. He only chanced to see the light from her room suddenly falling like a square on the carpet. Miss Buckley came out of her room in a hurry and went quickly to Mr. Wilbur's door and opened it with a key. She went inside, closing his door behind her. She had never once looked in Mr. Greene's direction.

Mr. Greene in his anger nearly lost control of himself, but he waited a full minute, then went back to Twelve, inserted his passkey, and flung open the door. Miss Buckley was sitting on the bed, holding Mr. Wilbur and rocking from side to side, muttering to him. Mr. Wilbur was babbling words that Mr. Greene could not make out, staring at the foot of the bed.

Miss Buckley looked at Mr. Greene and went on holding Mr. Wilbur in her arms. "He gets these nightmares," she said.

6

The Retirement Blues

by EDWARD STREETER

In the fictional excerpt that follows, we see a picture of an individual, Mr. Crombie, facing the prospect of forced retirement. Through his voice and those of his wife and friends, we perceive some of the economic, social, and psychological adjustments that retirement can necessitate for some people.

THEY WERE ALL seated around the long table in the new gray-paneled board room. Bingham, head of bond investments, was holding forth on money rates. So they hadn't waited for him after all! . . .

INTERACTION, DECEMBER 1973

A man like Mr. Crombie might not find much comfort in the thought that he could do RSVP work after retirement. But, in fact, the satisfaction to be derived from doing small, useful tasks like fixing a toaster might go a long way toward dispelling his retirement despondency.

Did all these men realize that within a year and a half he, Graham Crombie, the man who had put this show on the road, was going to retire? Was he the only one who had not taken that clause in the pension plan seriously? Of course he was. Everyone else had been aware of his retirement date for months. Their interest was not in him, however, but rather in the degree of benefit that might accrue to each as a result of his withdrawal. . . .

* * *

It might be nearer the truth to admit that he had never expected the rule to apply to *him*. He had been like a soldier charging across a field swept by machine-gun fire. Those singing bullets were meant for other men.

This was all his leaping mind needed to put on a brand-new scene. He was entering the board room. He recognized the principal department heads and the investment specialists. Gleason occupied the chair at the head of the table. "Graham," he said, as all eyes turned toward Mr. Crombie, "this is a revolt. We've just had a meeting and we've decided that no matter *what* the pension plan says you can't retire. This business *needs* you too much. We *all* need you, Graham. You're at the peak of your form, and you've got to stay on. You're *drafted!*"

There were shouts of approval. Miss Parkinson, whom he had not noticed before, was crying and waving her notebook. Then this gratifying sequence was replaced by Jinny standing in the hall of the apartment. "I'll be so glad when you step out of this whole rat race."

They all took it for granted. There would be no revolt. The whole office had undoubtedly been discussing it for months. He suddenly felt sorry for himself.

How in the world was he going to finance retirement? Had anybody thought of that? No. And what was more, they cared less. He had spent the best part of his life building up a successful business and, now that they were all assured of their fat salaries, they were going to toss him out on a minor technicality, to starve or sell apples or whatever appealed to him in his new-found freedom.

He'd never saved much money. It had always come so easily that there had been no reason to suppose this pleasant condition would ever cease. Jinny had recently received some money from her father's estate. Thank heaven for that, although it was no fortune. Rather decent of the old fellow, though, to expire so unselfishly at just the right moment.

Perhaps the company might give him a retaining fee as a consultant. He turned this idea over in his mind for several minutes. Then he remembered Sam Bunker. Sam had been one of the first to retire after the pension plan went into effect, and they had retained him as a consultant partly because he had been one of the best market analysts in the Street, and partly because, being unaccustomed at that time to compulsory retirement, it had seemed too brutal to push him out after all his years with the company. There was no question that Bunker *had* been a great analyst, but as soon as he retired he seemed to lose touch with the current picture and based all his judgments on a past that had no application to the modern world.

That wasn't the heart of the trouble, however. The young fellows who were coming up behind him wouldn't have taken Bunker's advice had he been the Delphic Oracle. To have done so, quite obviously, would have meant that they were in *need* of advice. So the old fellow just became a damn nuisance, hanging around people's desks when they were busy. They had a dreadful time getting rid of him. Mr. Crombie dismissed the idea of being a consultant to his own company.

Perhaps the company would grant him a supplemental pension. There was nothing to prevent it. Then he remembered old Conrad. Old Conrad was an economist. He'd shown considerable promise in the early days, when Crombie, Hamilton, and Gardiner was still a small partnership. But the man lacked drive. He just never *got* anywhere. Nice enough fellow—a gentleman and all that—but he lacked what it took.

One morning Miss Parkinson had come to him looking upset. "Mr. Conrad's outside," she said. "He's retiring next month, you know. He wants to see you about something in connection with his pension. I told him you were busy, but he said it was important." She shrugged, as much as to say, "What can you do with people like that?"

"Never too busy to see one of my boys," Crombie had replied. He said it loud enough so that Conrad, standing in the outer office, could hear. "Come in, Conrad. Come in. Don't stand on ceremony in this office."

Old Conrad had shuffled in and sat down on the edge of Mr. Crombie's leather-cushioned visitor's chair. He didn't know what to do with his hands. Mr. Crombie had felt like loaning him his hat so that he could turn it slowly while he talked.

There had been an awkward silence. "Well, Conrad, I hear you're about to retire," Mr. Crombie had said by way of a self-starter.

"That's what I came to see you about, sir. I suppose you'll think it's very impertinent of me, but my wife said I owed it to my family to talk to you."

"You can always talk to me, Conrad. You know that. The door to this office is never shut."

"I know, sir. And it's appreciated. But this is rather an unusual situation." He had hesitated, his fingers working nervously on the arms of the chair. "You see, sir, I've never had what you might call a big salary, so that now, when I put my pension and my Social Security together, it comes to only a little over $3,000 a year. I might be able to live on that if it wasn't for my wife. She's an invalid and needs quite a bit of medical care."

Mr. Crombie remembered remorsefully the wave of irritation that had swept over him. It was not due to any lack of sympathy, but rather because old Conrad was about to present him with a dilemma for which he had no solution. It put him in the position of having devised a pension plan so inadequate that men couldn't live on it.

"Do you own a home?" he asked, largely for something to say.

"Yes, sir, in a way. There's a mortgage on it."

"How many children do you have?"

"Two, sir. They're married, and I guess they can take care of themselves."

"Couldn't they help you out a little?"

"Oh, no, sir. They've got five kids between them and neither of them earns much. They just about make the grade and that's all. You know how it is."

Mr. Crombie had drummed thoughtfully on the desk with his fingertips. The trouble with Conrad was, and had always been, that he didn't have common sense or judgment or whatever it was. Pension plans had been created to *supplement* a man's savings, not to support him, without any further contribution on his part, for the rest of his life. Perhaps the whole pension idea was a mistake that merely sapped people's self-reliance and made them think the world owed them a living.

"Conrad," he had said, and he still remembered what a heel he had felt as he listened to his own words—but what other course could he have taken? The plan was there, rigid, legalized, certainly not something that could be regulated like a water faucet. "I wish I could help. I hope you know that. But, as you are well aware, our plan is set up to give each employee a certain sum of money on retirement, based on years of service and salary. It's a hard and fast formula. Now, you're too good an economist to think that we can change that formula at will. If we did it for one, we'd have to do it for all, and the whole plan would be on the scrap pile. You understand that, don't you, Conrad?"

"Of course, sir. I shouldn't have spoken about it. It was my wife. I wish I hadn't." He fumbled uneasily with his chin.

"No, Conrad. Don't feel that way. I'm glad you did speak, and I want you to explain to your wife just how this thing is set up. Have you ever thought about selling that house of yours and buying yourself a little place in some lovely spot like Vermont—a small house with some ground around it, where you could grow vegetables and keep a chicken or two?

"After people know you, you might even get a job in the local bank or post office or something. This is a real challenge, Conrad—and I think you're going to be a lot happier because you worked it out yourself.

"I'm not saying good-by to you now. I'll see you

before you go. But remember, this door is always open. You must keep in touch with your old friends."

That was obviously the exit line. They had both stood up. There were tears in old Conrad's eyes. "Thank you, sir," he had said. "You've been more than kind to me. I'll never forget it." They shook hands and he walked out of the office.

No, there would be no supplemental pension. He'd follow his own advice. They'd move to some little place in the country and lead a quiet existence, dropping out of the New York life entirely.

* * *

For the first time she [Mrs. Crombie] realized that he did not want to face the day when he was no longer boss-man of Crombie, Hamilton, and Gardiner. As a matter of fact, she did not want to, either. Over the years, she had created a way of life that was both stimulating and satisfactory. She had no desire to change any part of it. But when the routine of men like Graham Crombie was broken, things were bound to change.

What in the world did retired men do with themselves all day? Did they just sit around the apartment trying to keep out of the way of the cleaning women and asking their wives where they were going every time they put on their hats? What *was* there for the poor things to do?

* * *

Christmas came and went, then New Year's Day. The matter of Mr. Crombie's successor had not yet been decided, although everybody seemed to assume it would be Gleason and had been acting accordingly for months. Mr. Crombie began to have the gnawing feeling of frustration that comes with postponing something you know must be done.

He called up George Gillespie and asked him to lunch with him at the club. George had been retired almost a year. Like Mr. Crombie he had been the head of his own business. Above all he was a realist. There was no nonsense about George Gillespie. He said what he thought, and he usually thought straight.

"So it's caught up with you, too," he said, when the waiter had taken their order. "I'll bet you wrote yourself out of a job just the way I did. That old clause about mandatory retirement at sixty-five—I put it in myself."

"So did I," said Mr. Crombie, "and I still think I was right."

"Of course you were right from the company's point of view. But we were wrong from *our* point of view. Make retirement discretionary and every unimaginative old dodo in the shop wants to stay on. And the board will be sorry for them because they never seem to have enough money to live on, and there they'll be, like rocks in the middle of a stream; cantankerous old 'no' men, blocking promotion, sore because conditions are changing and, worst of all, quietly sabotaging new ideas at a time when every company's future depends on new ideas."

George Gillespie stared at his large, bony-fingered hands. They were becoming old man's hands, the veins showing and the skin loose on the backs. "No, Graham. I'm sorry to say that what's good for the company isn't necessarily good for you and me."

"That's what I want to talk to you about," said Mr. Crombie. "Haven't you been happy since you retired?"

"Hell, no," said Gillespie. "Listen, Graham, I

worked since the day I got out of college—forty-three years—not because I wanted to—at first, anyway—but because I had to. Then, like so many others, as I succeeded I began to like the racket more and more, until at last work became a part of me."

"I guess it was more or less the same with me," said Mr. Crombie.

"It's nothing to be ashamed of," Gillespie continued, "but modern business involves such an intensive kind of conditioning for those who want to succeed that after a while nothing else is quite real.

"That's why, when you fling a man out of his job at sixty-five, he's apt to sink, particularly if it's been a top job. Nobody wants him in the business world and he's been conditioned to look down his nose at anything outside of it."

"I know," said Mr. Crombie. "You'd think, though, that with all their experience the good men would be in demand after retirement. You'd think they'd be valuable at least in an advisory capacity."

"For the majority, the answer to that is 'nuts,' " said Gillespie, impatiently. "Sure, the specialists, the fellows who know things nobody else knows, the scientific boys—they're in demand, but not the general run of us. Take you, for instance: who the hell wants a guy like you?" Mr. Crombie hoped the glum-looking man eating alone behind him hadn't overheard. "Or me, either," added Gillespie, generously. "What specific knowledge have you got? You had something else, Graham. You had the gift of success, which is getting other people to work for you, and getting people to believe in you. You're a salesman, Graham, not a technician. It's fellows like you that build the businesses and make the money, but your resale value is nil.

"No, when guys like us are out, we're out. If we'd stayed on, some of us might have done a good job for quite some time. But on the average it's a good thing from the company's point of view to get rid of us at sixty-five."

"But lots of people have interests outside their businesses," protested Mr. Crombie, looking distressed. "You talk as if all businessmen were mentally muscle-bound. You had interests. A lot of them. Aren't you following them up?"

"The trouble is, Graham, fellows like us are too busy to really plan what we're going to do when we retire—too busy to get ready for it. Sure, I had interests, but I never developed them. They never got past the 'interests' state. For instance, I always wanted to travel, but I never thought it through—never planned it intelligently. So what happens. Three days after I pull out of business we get on board a floating hotel and away we go. Where? Anywhere. No need to tie ourselves down to schedules any more—we were going to take a year, go around the world, perhaps, but in our own time and in our own way. Hell, at the end of six months we never wanted to see another hotel. At the end of eight we never wanted to see each other. At the end of nine we came home.

"People who enjoy business and who have been lucky enough to be successful don't plan retirement, partly because we're too busy, partly because we don't want to believe that anybody else can do the job we've been doing, and so we hope we're going to be drafted to stay on—and then there's a third reason. It's the same one that applies to people who can't bring themselves to make a will. Retirement has always been synonymous with old age—with slowing down. The idea of slowing down makes people like us sick. Q.E.D.: just plow ahead until to your surprise and indignation some pension plan gives the signal and they pull the trap door on you."

"You talk as if you didn't like pension plans," said Mr. Crombie.

"Well, I wouldn't put it that way. They're giving people security in their old age that they never had before. But you can't have your cake and eat it too. You have to pay for all that security somehow. You pay for it two ways. A pension plan can shackle a guy to a job. What happens if he works for a company with a pension plan for forty years and then gets an offer of a better job in another company? He can't carry his pension benefits with him the way a turtle lugs his shell around, and he can't afford to throw away all those accumulated benefits and start all over again at the bottom of the totem pole, even though he might be getting a lot bigger salary. With taxes where they are, what chance has he to lay by anything?

"That applies more to old codgers like you and me than to the young fellows. They're smarter—bolder. When they get offered a big job they don't think about pension plans or salary any more. They think in terms of stock options, and they've got confidence in themselves to make them good. You know all about that.

"The other way you pay for your damned security is having to get out when you're sixty-five. I suppose some are only too glad to have the excuse. But a lot of them aren't. Personally, I think we *ought* to be glad, in spite of the fact that I'm not. This little old world is changing faster than you and I can keep up with it. We had certain things drilled into us and we operated on those principles. These kids today wouldn't know what I'm talking about.

They're opportunists, not from choice, but because they have to be. You can't set your course and steer by it any more. Business today is more like a slalom race where, in the middle of the run, somebody's changed the flags. You've either got to respond fast or you'll be out of the race. You and I are pulling out at the right time, Graham, even though we don't know it. This is no world for pontificating, pompous old men. It's a world for broken-field runners—a young man's world. The only trouble is it leaves me all dressed up with no place to go."

* * *

The duties and obligations that he had complained of so bitterly suddenly began to appear in a new light now that he was about to be relieved of them. The great dinners at the Waldorf at which his firm was always browbeaten into taking a table or into helping some business associate to fill his, the luncheons in the private dining rooms of exclusive clubs or (depending on the tastes of the customer) in the more relaxed atmosphere of "21," the night ball games in the company's box halfway between home plate and first, the noise and confusion of conventions, the flying business trips about the country, the incessant committee and board meetings, the requests for favors that somehow must be granted, now appeared to him nostalgically in the soft amber light of his setting sun.

So many of these activities had acquired an unrealized social quality. The men with whom he had sat through the years on charitable and commercial boards, who had worked with him on club committees and on groups appointed to investigate and report on some hopeless muddle, had gradually become his friends. To some degree they had replaced his college and prebusiness connections.

As long as he was the active head of a large, sucessful company nothing would change. It was becoming disturbingly evident, however, that on the day he retired his status would suddenly shift from somebody to nobody: a person occupying no established place in the community, unwanted and unneeded, not because people didn't like him but because their financial attachment was to Crombie, Hamilton, and Gardiner, the institution, rather than to Graham Crombie, the man.

7

Fear Stalks the Elderly

by THOMAS C. FOX

The article that follows, which was part of an award-winning series on the elderly in Detroit, discusses three of their fears—violent crime, lack of consumer protection, and isolation. Although one might question to what extent all of the elderly experience each of these fears, there seems to be no denying that each one is of concern to many.

WHEN Marie Munch, eighty-one, was stabbed to death on her bed in her two-story brick home three weeks ago, she became the twelfth person over sixty to be slain by intruding robbers in Detroit this year.

First published as "Fears Stalk Elderly Residents," by Thomas C. Fox, the *Detroit Free Press*, June 19, 1973. Reprinted by permission of the *Detroit Free Press*.

JOHN McENROE

The reinforced glass and the burglar alarms in the door and windows of the building in this photo remind us that many older Americans live in poor neighborhoods where crime rates are high.

tion's aged are the number-one target for an almost limitless variety of con games and frauds."

It listed "home repairs," "debt adjusting," "chain referral selling," "dance studio rackets," "model home swindles," and the "pigeon-drop swindle" as some of the most common schemes by which the elderly are "bilked of hundreds of millions of dollars each year."

In addition, the elderly lose large parts of their savings by more legal methods.

A recent confidential study by the U.S. Senate Small Business Subcommittee revealed that pharmaceutical firms soak older Americans and other patients up to thirty times too much for lifesaving drugs. The elderly use more drugs collectively than any other segment of the population.

"At the heart of the problem is the lack of transportation," Margaret Hossack, director of the Mayor's Senior Citizens Commission, said recently. "The senior citizens are simply not able to get around, compare prices, and find out what things really cost. So they become easy victims."

She added that many con men play on the loneliness of the elderly by listening sympathetically to them before peddling their schemes.

In Detroit, the Mayor's Senior Citizens Commission has laid the groundwork for a nutrition program for the elderly. It would establish perhaps as many as forty centers where senior citizens could gather to eat and associate with friends. But federal funding for this program has been held up for several years already.

Dr. Eve Kahana, a gerontologist at Wayne State University, recently investigated the lives of some elderly persons living alone to see what they felt their needs are.

"I was surprised at first to find," she said, "that one of the most pressing needs older people feel is the proper care of their feet."

She explained that her finding really should not have been so startling, saying that for many elderly persons, their feet become a symbol of their mobility.

"If their feet break down, they see themselves losing their mobility—and translated, it means increased isolation."

Figures show that 8 percent of Detroit's elderly are bedridden. Twenty-seven percent more are ambulatory but ill, and thus their movements are somewhat curtailed.

[illegible]

AGING, FEBRUARY-MARCH 1970

These older people share responsibilities and enjoy each other's company in a congregate in a small Nebraska town.

who are sixty-five years or older, and one-third of them are over seventy-six. Most insurance companies today expect men to live to seventy and women to seventy-three. One of these days, most of us are going to have to face the fact that we are old.

What then? The familiar alternatives are these: retirement complexes or homes, hotels for the elderly, nursing homes, living with children or other relatives, or struggling to somehow do it yourself. Most of us know the problems of each of these alternatives, and this knowledge surely adds to our fear of aging. Who wants to live out the last days alone, in a shabby hotel or old apartment, eating irregularly and not well? How many people can afford to move into retirement complexes, where founders' fees and monthly maintenance bills are often exorbitant and where the activities seem geared to keeping us young, rather than letting us grow old with grace? How many parents really want to, or *can,* live with their own children without feeling like a burden and experiencing the crankiness that results? Who wants to end up in what President Nixon, referring to nursing homes, called "dumping grounds for the dying" or "warehouses for the unwanted"? There is a necessity for nursing homes, of course; some people need the medical attention and constant care they provide. But often people are put in nursing homes simply because there is no place else for them to go.

There is a new alternative, too, or—at least—a successful model. For the past two years, up to eighteen senior citizens at a time, ranging in age from seventy to ninety-five, have been living as a family in Winter Park, Florida. Along with a middle-aged couple and the couple's children and grandchildren, these elderly people have joined together to share a home. It is a home where they can live their lives as they want to, with dignity and love, where they can care for, help, and argue with each other, and where they can participate in as much or as little work as they want.

Joe McInerny, a distinguished-looking seventy-six-year-old man with a black patch over one eye, has been living in the Winter Park house almost a year. When Calvin Coolidge was vice-president, McInerny was his chauffeur. Afterward, McInerny worked for the FBI, then as a private investigator for the government. Upon retiring, he lived alone in Connecticut, then went to Florida for a vacation and decided to stay. He lived by himself until his health failed, and he had to go into a nursing home and, later, to a hospital. When McInerny was about to be released from the hospital, his son, who lives in Chicago, came to Florida to help him find a place to live. They located the Winter Park family, and McInerny moved into the twenty-seven-room house set on three acres of lakeside land.

When McInerny feels like talking about the old days now, or about his son and grandchildren, he can usually find someone who is eager to listen and learn. That's a lot different, he says, from the way it was in the nursing home. Living here, McInerny is also able to come and go as he pleases. Usually he eats at one of the two large tables in the dining room; sometimes he goes out with friends to seafood restaurants. When he wakes up in the morning, a pot of coffee is always ready for him. When he wants privacy to watch television in his room, or look through his personal scrapbook, he has it. When he wants company, he has that, too.

Life in the house is quiet and comfortable. "We're all accomplished loafers, and we know how to enjoy our loafing," says eighty-five-year-old Jess Bush. She likes to read—Conrad, Dickens, and detective stories—and to play Yahtzee, a dice game. Hulda Simonson, eighty-two, spends a lot of her time taming squirrels in the garden. There are trips to Florida's tourist attractions, and there is the freedom to help out around the home whenever someone feels up to it. Berta Almand, seventy-one, often cooks her southern specialties for the group.

There is the laughter of young people, too, the children and grandchildren of Jim Gillies, the house manager. Everyone is called "aunt" or "uncle" by the children and by each other, and Aunt Jess has been chosen by the family to be its nominal head. "I was drawn from the lot," she says, "because I talk more than most of the people here, and I keep an eye on them and get them things if they ask me to. And, also, I have a good memory. Some of the members of the family are forgetful sometimes, but here we don't think of it as senility, as they do in nursing homes. We really don't have difficulties with things like that here. Everyone forgets something sometimes, but we don't mind."

A kindly, well-spoken woman who was once secretary and bursar of Hunter College in New York, Aunt Jess is always ready to listen to problems and mediate arguments. "Old people can be difficult," she says. "I think the key to our success here has been Mr. Gillies. He has an optimistic disposition and a way of convincing you that every problem can be solved with cooperation."

Unlike standard retirement homes, where the rent often rises, the contribution is stable at the Winter Park place. Depending upon their financial states, the members' contributions range from $200 to $375 a month, as compared to $800 and up each month for a room in a decent nursing home. The contribution covers a monthly payment of $800 to the previous owner of the house (the family now holds the deed), heat, utilities, food, laundry, field trips, transportation—everything the family members need, except for personal items such as medicine, clothing, and meals out. It also covers food and lodging for any guests the family members wish to bring to their home.

The idea for this type of home came from forty-seven-year-old Jim Gillies, the house manager. Formerly, he was a salesman for food chains, and his work included catering the food for a dozen nursing homes in central Florida. In 1969, with the idea of starting up a different kind of home for elderly people, Gillies found and leased the house where the Winter Park family now lives. It had been a nursing home and had a wing equipped for the elderly—with ramps, railings, sit-down showers, sprinkler systems, and calling bells. Gillies moved in with his wife, four of their eight children, and three grandchildren. Four days later, their first "aunt" joined them. Within two months, three more "aunts," including Jess Bush, came to the family.

Eventually, as the family grew, Gillies had an attorney draw up articles for the Share-a-Home Association of Winter Park, Florida, an incorporated association consisting of the "aunts" and "uncles." These articles were finalized in May 1970, and amended in September 1971.

According to the articles, the members share a common ownership in the home and all the facilities of the home. They have the right to hire or fire a manager and assistant manager whose duties include providing food, lodging, and other needed services for the members of the association. The manager, who must post a $10,000 bond for himself, also takes care of the finances of the home. Additionally, he is responsible for providing transportation, laundry services, and medical attention for the members, and three regular meals a day for members and their guests.

Members must provide a power of attorney to a person of their choice to act in their behalf if they become incapacitated. They must be ambulatory—able to move about with or without mechanical devices. New members are chosen by the manager and have a thirty-day trial period before becoming full members of the association. During this time, any of the full members may bring up any objections they might have about the proposed member. The articles also provide for all new members to receive equity in the association, and for members who withdraw to be reimbursed for any payments made and not used.

The manager, Gillies, is paid $650 each month, plus room and board for himself and his family. His twenty-eight-year-old daughter Charlotte receives an additional $240 each month. Charlotte and Gillies' wife, who receives no salary, are responsible, with the help of another young woman, for general housekeeping, including housework, cooking, and laundry.

The arrangement has worked out so well that a group of Winter Park citizens has formed "Share-a-Home of America Inc.," a nonprofit corporation now collecting money to subsidize memberships in other homes it hopes will be founded on the Gillies plan. Three other homes are in the planning stage and another in Orange County, Florida, should soon open its doors.

The only major problem the family has had so far has been a court battle. A few months ago the members were served with subpoenas saying that they were in violation of the zoning laws regarding family dwellings. The members maintained that they fit within the law's definition of family—"one or more persons occupying a dwelling and living as a single housekeeping unit"—and after six hours of courtroom testimony and a personal visit to the home, Judge Claude Edwards of Florida's Ninth Circuit Court ruled in their favor.

"In court, I was afraid that it might be a paper operation," the judge said. "But then I went out and saw they were living as a family and as a single housekeeping unit. I was delighted to see that it was a happy, well-run family. There are so many lonely, alienated old people who lead restricted, unhappy, unproductive lives alone, because they would rather die than go into an institution. I think this is an answer to this type of problem. It is a superb idea."

9

Loneliness in a Nursing Home

by FRANCES AVERY FAUNCE

The following selection concentrates on the loneliness of women in a nursing home, but its implications are much broader, for loneliness is a feeling that affects many older people at one time or another, whether or not they live in nursing homes.

JUST WHAT is this loneliness of the nursing-home patient? This question was asked me searchingly by a friend whose mother and mother-in-law were both in homes. It is true that a nursing-home patient may be justifiably lonely and is almost certainly lonely in fact. The loneliness of the nursing-home patient is a compound of elements naturally varying with the

From *The Nursing Home Visitor*, by Frances Avery Faunce.

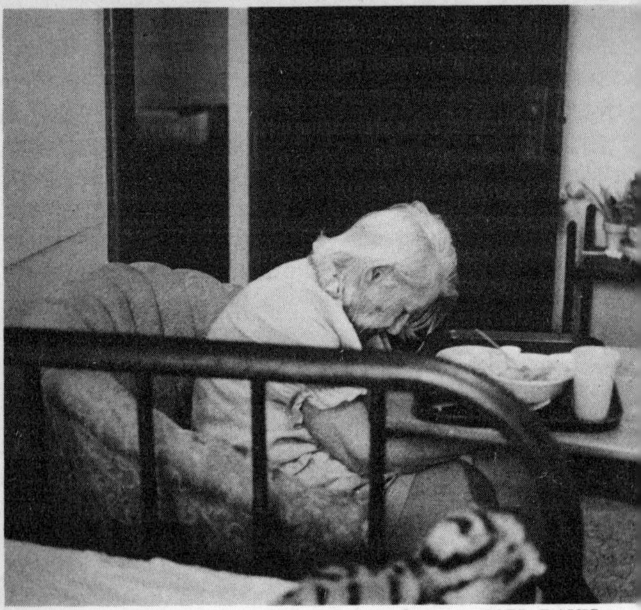

JOEL DAVIS

The feeling of aloneness often experienced by older people can be even more acute in the unfamiliar surroundings of a nursing home.

individual, but it is a feeling of lost-ness, of awayness from all that has been near and dear in an active life, of blank isolation from the past. The whole experience of this change into nursing-home life can create a state of shock in the elderly woman —in her mind and her spirit, causing nervous reactions that play on the functional and even organic states of the body. In this chapter it seems essential to spell out quite frankly some of the frequent causes of this basic shock. . . .

Lonely and *afraid* are two words commonly linked together, both in the mind that remains clear and in

er what might be the experience of an
ent whose husband has died. Shortly
falls and breaks her hip. From the
omes to the nursing home, for she has
ig cared for in her own house. She has
no relative or friend with whom she
has had to face the fact that this is
rmanent arrangement. She may be one
ho feel resentful at "having to come to
t seems as though she were confronted
ing that could make anybody sick."
of health, it is difficult to "count her
she is urged to do—difficult to focus
home offers by way of compensation.
t six of her likely difficulties.

EF. Loneliness for a longtime compan-
ral deterrent to settling peacefully into
-this strange room in this strange build-
husband never saw, never graced with
The patient has been wrenched from
ociations: "his" chair by the reading
ting that "he" might walk through some
, if she were only there. He has doubly
er life.

are date-minded feel a fresh grief on
You hear a widow say, "This would
ir sixtieth wedding anniversary today,"
band died seven years ago today," or,
birthday, and Jack always used to do
' Even her happy memories come back
tinge of sadness that, with some women,
om year to year to outweigh the truly
ations with the past.

ICKNESS. Let us say that this widow has
me under advice, to help pay for her

the mind of the patient who is "no longer herself." A woman who had come to convalesce from a hospital experience declared to me with fright in her face and gloom in her voice: "Oh, I am so lonely, so afraid!" And within a few days' time, another woman who had lived in this Home for some years, while her mind was gradually failing, whispered to me the same refrain, "I am so lonely, so afraid!" A social worker in geriatrics has told me that in all her experience she has found only a few people "on the outside" who were really aware of the despair suffered by many patients. One patient put it mildly, if sarcastically, when she commented, "It isn't exactly thrilling just to sit here."

This feeling of loneliness is not necessarily filled with bitterness, resentment, or envy, or marked by extreme despondency, though these signs may also appear. But even to a naturally cheerful person loneliness can be a terrible void—a hollowness of time and space and circumstance that nothing suffices to fill. "My stomach feels hollow" phrases it. And this hollowness affects the appetite, the digestion, sleep, deep breathing, the disposition. It may well be that we as patients are oppressed by the recognition that we are a problem to ourselves and to others—a problem that we are not ready or able to solve the way we want it solved. Until or unless we come to the happy point of accepting things in life as they are where we are now having to live it, we inwardly want to turn back the clock to remembered days.

Let me set down here a variety of causes [of loneliness] as they might be confessed by one or another patient whose adjustment is disturbed. Most of these statements I myself have heard:

1. "The dullness of Sunday afternoon when many of the others have visits from relatives or friends, but I don't."

2. "Several successive days with no one coming to see me."

3. "No mail for me, when it is being taken around to my neighbors."

4. "The fact that my hearing has now failed so that I can't listen to the radio or even enjoy television, and I can't enter into group conversation."

5. "Not being able to get into a car any longer so that I have to recognize that I am housebound."

6. "Having such a small space of my own, and without the many things I've always enjoyed in my home."

7. "Lack of regular work such as housekeeping, so that I feel I'm not of any use any more. I'm not really wanted anywhere."

8. "I'm haunted by the finality of it all. Does this mark the end of my ever again living in a home with a small *h?*"

9. "Even with assistance, have I money enough to carry me through?"

10. "I have the feeling not of having everything taken away from me, but of my being taken away from everything."

11. "It's too much to expect me to adapt myself to a new routine with everything so strange and different." . . .

In contrast, elderly
and mental health fo
in their own homes a
always done, however

The fact that th
longer than that o
larger number of w
of these patients ar
in which the wife
in their home, wit
Then her loss, whe
longed illness, may
and soon unable t
needs. Possibly a y
for a shorter or lon
scores of variable
cannot last indefinite
cerned may be, a va
ing home.

Let's consi
imagined pat
afterward she
hospital she c
no way of bei
no children,
can live. She
probably a p
of the many
this." To her
with "everyt
In her state
blessings," a
on what the
Let us look

1. HER GR
ion is a natu
this new life-
ing the "lost
his presence
precious ass
table, the fee
familiar doo
gone out of
Many wh
special days
have been c
or, "My hu
"This is my
this or that.
with a deep
continues f
joyful associ

2. HOME
sold her h

new expenses. Her furniture has been dispersed; possibly some has been put in storage. As the saying goes, her home has been "broken up," and she has to work hard not to feel broken up herself when she dwells on memories of the old environment. She misses the familiar views from her former windows. Her small room seems cramped, and she may have to share it with one or more other patients. She longs for the friendly neighbors and the postman she had for so many years. She is restless to get back and work in her garden. She misses housekeeping and being mistress of her own domain.

These wishes to be back again involve the emotional hardship of accepting the fact that running the old home demanded health no longer at her command. To be robbed of these old joys calls for tremendous patience and courage and, as we shall see later, purposeful imagination to fill life with new kinds of satisfying joy.

In a nursing home, she may have a precious photograph standing on her table. She may be allowed to have her own easy chair from home. But the routine is "not like home," not like family life. The sights and sounds are strange.

With all these varying factors, one aspect of "feeling homesick" is easily overlooked; yet it is possibly the most important of all. A widow (and for that matter any woman) misses her own former self at this point. Such a break in life's pattern undercuts self-respect, and this is one of the foundation stones of contentment and security. The patient may feel that she wouldn't have to stay here in this unwanted environment *if only she could find herself.* She readily imagines her former younger self moving about the old home. As a woman's mind fails, if it does, she may be one of the many who keep wanting to pack a suitcase to go home. That suitcase of hers, she may not realize, was not left at the nursing home; the relative who brought her knew that her traveling days were over.

3. LOSS OF OUTSIDE CONTACTS. If the widow is well advanced in years, it may well be that few if any of her contemporaries are able to come to see her. She may have no younger relative to keep running in, and her busy younger friends will not often find time to visit her. If she is no longer able to get into a car, she cannot enjoy the change of going out for a drive or to church or to see friends. Perhaps she can't go shopping any more!

4. LOSS OF HER HEALTH. We are thinking of a woman whose mind is still clear enough to understand her situation, but who is lacking in vigor and may be in pain. If her sight and hearing are impaired, she doesn't really enjoy television or radio. She feels remote from the world of newspapers, magazines, books.

5. FINANCIAL INSECURITY. The widow may be haunted by the fear that her money won't hold out, even with the help of agencies. She may be uncertain for many months as to where she does "stand" until her husband's estate is settled. Even if relatives and friends are generous in helping to cover any financial gap, the widow is conscious of now being a dependent for the first time since childhood.

6. USELESSNESS. The other night a recently widowed patient explained to me: "I don't want to go to bed early, but I'm tired of doing nothing." Even though there may be occupational therapy or occasionally guided handwork, there are many idle hands. Permanent leisure is not the luxury one

might suppose. To be useful is wonderfully stabilizing. "I'm not of any use anymore; nobody needs me," cries the patient. This is the heart of it, until the patient is able to find herself as an integral part of the nursing home "family." Then service to others, however slight, can be absorbing. One who has this inferior feeling, as though she had been demoted, needs to be helped to the assurance that she has gained security and good care that compensate for many of the things she wishes to be, to have, and to do. And besides, there *are* constructive ways of service that lead to contentment.

Too often, widow or not, the woman who enters the nursing home is "the last leaf on the tree"—without any kin or anyone who can come to see her or even communicate with her in any way. An appeal could be hung over many a bed: "Wanted: a niece!"

With the passage of months, many patients have to meet poignant losses of relatives and friends. News of the death of one or another contemporary is not unusual. . . .

It is true that some cases go in and then out of nursing homes as convalescent, but for many women the loneliness is intensified because they know that they may be, as they say, "in for life." . . . Only last week, I heard a woman sigh that she has nothing to live for, that no one comes to see her, that she doesn't know whether her money will hold out, that she isn't afraid to die, but she doesn't want to die in a Home with a capital *H*. This bundle of fears is not unusual.

AGING, SEPTEMBER 1971

President Nixon visits patients in a nursing home in New Hampshire. Politicians are not unaware that the elderly represent a powerful voting bloc. If older Americans were better organized, their political power would be formidable.

10

Nursing-Home Hearings

by THE SUBCOMMITTEE ON LONG-TERM CARE OF THE SPECIAL COMMITTEE ON AGING, U.S. SENATE

During 1971, a subcommittee of the U.S. Senate held hearings in Chicago, as they previously had in other cities. The Chicago hearings were preceded by an investigation of nursing homes in that city by a citizens' watchdog group and by reporters from the **Chicago Tribune.** The following excerpts from the hearings reveal some of the conditions these investigators discovered and also show the concern of politicians and private citizens over the abuses so often found.

Statement of Senator Charles H. Percy

SENATOR PERCY: Mr. Chairman, I thank you very much and I welcome you here, and I know Senator Stevenson joins me in welcoming you to Chicago.

We bring you here because we feel that some of the conditions that exist in nursing homes in Chicago and other parts of the state are typical of some of the circumstances we find across the country. It is the purpose of the U.S. Senate and this particular committee to try to determine what we can do about these conditions, because we have a very real responsibility.

We come to Chicago because one of our newspapers and the news media have developed a body of evidence, together with the Better Government Association, that gives us an insight that goes far beyond the insight that we can get in any other city in the United States today.

We know, for instance, that patients in nursing homes are not receiving high-quality care despite massive infusions of state and federal funds.

. . . [We] just came from a home that was old, in run-down condition, that provided a dismal surrounding for people who have been consigned to what might be called a warehouse. It is so typical of many of the older structures where we leave our senior citizens.

Substandard homes are being licensed or are being closed and then quickly reopened for some reason, despite repeated and flagrant violations of the health, safety, and housing standards, and this condition exists across the country.

We find unqualified personnel mistreating patients and dispensing drugs about which they know nothing. These are conditions that we know exist now.

Patients are being immobilized, instead of rehabilitated, through the use of heavy sedation, and the point system frequently provides incentive for the owners of nursing homes to have people bedridden rather than up out of bed, because they get paid more if the people are in poor health and have bed-sores than if they are well.

We wonder why this system is permitted to exist.

We do know that there are shared responsibilities on all levels of government. Every level of government must review the degree to which it is fulfilling its responsibility to the elderly, and that means the federal government as well as the state and local governments.

The diffusion of responsibility itself is very confusing and suggests that the relationship between various levels of government should receive more of our attention.

In addition to examining the roles of these governmental agencies, we should also ask a number of other important questions during these hearings.

Are the standards for nursing-home administrators, nurses, and other employees adequate, or should they be upgraded?

Are the court procedures reasonable that one must follow to close a home that is clearly substandard?

Is the state's policy of transferring mental patients into nursing homes good or bad?

How adequate is the medical supervision given to nursing-home patients?

How important is the profit motive in taking care of the elderly?

* * *

I believe that our hospitals that take care of the young and the middle-aged across the country are not essentially set up for profit, and yet of twenty-five thousand nursing homes for the elderly, 90 percent are set up for profit, are privately owned as investments.

What is the rate of return on these investments? How much are these people making on the poor? When we consider that the revenue of these homes is $2.5 billion a year, this is a multibillion dollar business—$1.8 billion comes from the federal government. It is our responsibility to find out whether or not this system itself is right and proper.

We would like to take Illinois as a laboratory and find out who owns these homes, how many other homes they own, if there are interlocking directorates.

Is there a conglomeration here of ownership and almost, you might say, a conspiracy to exploit the poor? We have the power in the Senate of the United States to get the facts. We have the responsibility to bring these facts to light so that if everything is all right, fine—but if it is not, let's find out what we can do about it.

As we attempt to find answers to these questions, we should be wary of falling into the easy trap of fixing the blame on any one individual or group.

What these hearings are not intended to do is to issue a blanket indictment of the nursing-home industry or of officials from any given level of government.

There may be profiteering nursing-home operators, and there may be inept city, state, and federal officials, but I think we must not lose sight of the fact that there are also many fine homes and many honest, sincere individuals dedicated to the improvement of health care for the elderly.

A final but crucial issue that we must consider during these hearings is society's attitude toward the elderly.

Hearings on nursing homes have been held before, and investigations and studies have been conducted. Legislation to remedy some of the problems has been passed, and efforts to enforce the new laws have been increased. . . .

I am convinced, however, that no number of hearings or investigations or studies or new laws will put an end to the suffering and human misery so prevalent in our homes for the aged unless and until we reexamine our basic attitude toward older people.

Statement of William Recktenwald, Investigator, BGA

MR. RECKTENWALD: My name is William Recktenwald, and I am an investigator for the Better Government Association.

We are grateful that this committee has come to Chicago for a firsthand look at nursing-home abuses. This problem has received our complete attention for more than three months.

You have already heard from the families of some of the victims of nursing-home neglect. They are a few of the hundreds of persons who have come forward in recent weeks—each one with a new and more sickening story of what is happening to our most helpless minority—the elderly poor.

For three months, working in cooperation with the *Chicago Tribune,* we watched this helpless minority spend their final days in wretched despair.

Working as mop boys, nurse's aides, and janitors, we saw garbage scraped from one tray to another to make meager food supplies go around. We were told to administer drugs and medication within hours after we obtained employment using phony job references that were never checked.

We saw elderly patients struck and kicked because they dared to complain or cried out for mercy.

In one case, an investigator seeking work as a janitor was hired as a nursing-home administrator by an absentee owner who was trying to get the health department off his back.

We saw filth and vermin so overwhelming that in one of the city's largest homes the night staff has surrendered large areas of the building to rats.

I worked in four of these homes and posed as a mentally retarded patient in a fifth. Time after time, I saw the so-called golden years become a grim death sentence in places where nobody cares.

I watched a ninety-one-year-old man, his legs weakened by age, beg for gentle care as two aides attempted to give him a bath. Their response was all too typical of the poorly paid employees of these warehouses for the dying—they slapped him across the face, and he fell into the tub.

11

On Aging

by JAMES WOOD

How can the young learn about the old? The article below seems to indicate a number of good methods, one of the best being the utilization of older people as resource leaders in teaching the young about aging. Perhaps if ageism and stereotyping are to be overcome, efforts like the ones described here will have to become more common.

THE Presentation High School girls wore dark plastic glasses, the kind you use when your eyes are dilated for a vision test. Their ears were plugged with cotton, and their fingertips were wrapped with two layers of masking tape, impeding their sense of touch.

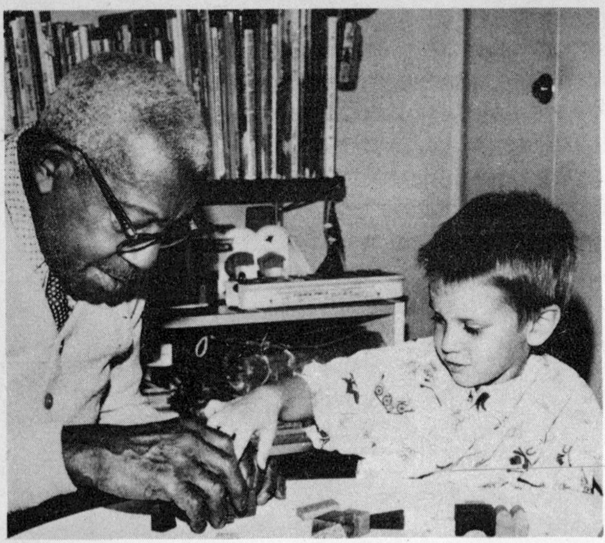

INTERACTION, DECEMBER 1973

The Foster Grandparent Program fills gaps in the lives of both young and old.

These San Francisco high-school seniors were learning what old people go through as they begin to lose their faculties. What gradually became clear as the girls continued talking was that they could, in fact, cope with their "disabilities." The experience, which taught the girls that old people are not necessarily ready to be put on a shelf and forgotten, was part of a new Youth and Aging Curriculum implemented in three Catholic high schools in San Francisco.

Attempting to mediate in the war of the generations, the program has won the praise of youth and senior citizens alike. However, its originator, social worker Marie Malveaux, conceded that there were a minicourse between regular class terms, or integrated into the curriculum of various courses, it had a strong impact on the students. Of 214 students who took the course, 201 answered on a questionnaire that they thought the course was worthwhile. A sizable majority, 162, said that they thought the course should be given in miniform, that is, in one to three weeks of intensive study, including field trips, conferences, and interviews with resource persons.

Ms. Malveaux believes the student reactions show that teenagers are receptive to knowledge about aging and that they welcome contact with older persons in the classroom. The experience enriches the lives of both the young and the old.

As one student who took the course wrote: "Growing old is part of your life, different from the rest. Your surroundings are different, your reactions —everything you do is different.

"It is a new way of living. You might be more comfortable and happy, or you might dislike being old. But whether or not you like it, you can find ways to cope with it."

AGING, DECEMBER 1968

The free or low-cost bus service for senior citizens that is provided by many communities can help make the difference between an isolated, miserable old age and a sociable, pleasant one.

12

After 65: Resources for Self-Reliance

by THEODORE IRWIN

In the selection that follows, a number of the services that have recently become available to the elderly are pointed out. As a result of the 1973 amendments to the Older Americans Act, more such services should be forthcoming in the future.

THE CAPACITY of an older person to function at a decent level of health and well-being may depend largely on the community resources open to him. Traditionally, these have been fragmented among family service agencies, public welfare departments, community centers, churches, settlement houses. Currently, resources range from home nursing to

---

mobile meals, telephone calls to the homebound, friendly visitors, and day center facilities.

Such services are designed to supplement rather than substitute for family help. "Expansion of community social and health services," contends Elaine M. Brody, "can strengthen family ties and enable family members to maximize their functioning in meeting responsibilities to the elderly."

The Older Americans Act of 1965 gave considerable impetus to community planning for the elderly by authorizing funds to help establish and strengthen agencies on aging and to develop opportunities for older people. As a consequence, a wide diversity of demonstration projects were set up in such fields as legal aid, libraries, nutrition, transportation, homemaker service, and employment counseling.

These and other programs are tools with which to combat both the withdrawal from society by members of the older generation and their exclusion by our society. Yet these tools are still inadequate in many respects. In some communities, these resources do not exist at all; in others, they meet only a small part of the need.

A large segment of the aging population would pay a fee for needed services but are unable to acquire them for a fee they can afford. And even the reasonably affluent suffer when services are unavailable. But new provisions for the elderly are emerging. . . .

Day Centers for the Elderly

After her stroke, seventy-seven-year-old Myra Barrow became a burden to her daughter and son-in-law, whose home in Baltimore she was sharing.

Mrs. Barrow could move about to a limited extent, but needed help and rehabilitation. Her family felt she shouldn't be left alone; the constant demands on them were a strain.

Highly sensitive, Mrs. Barrow feared being put in a nursing home, which to her meant "the end," cut off from her beloved family. And her family was more than willing to keep her in their home—if somehow the pressures could be reduced.

The happy solution: day care at a Baltimore geriatric center and hospital. Each weekday morning, Mrs. Barrow and seven other older adults are picked up by a van-type vehicle fitted with a lift to accommodate those who would otherwise find it hard to step into it. At the center's affiliated hospital, she receives treatment from a physical therapist, following a program prescribed by her own doctor. A nurse is there to observe her, carry out the doctor's orders, and give her her medication on time.

During the day, Mrs. Barrow enjoys making afghans in arts and crafts, occasionally watches a movie, attends parties, listens to speakers on current events. She has gained new friends—men and women of her generation—many of whom have heart conditions or other serious physical handicaps. Mrs. Barrow has her special-diet lunch in the common dining room and a late-afternoon meal that further relieves the pressure on her daughter. In the evening, Mrs. Barrow returns home to her familiar bed. A social worker from the center occasionally visits the family.

Her daughter reports that Mrs. Barrow has improved remarkably. More talkative now, she always has something to relate when she comes home. She no longer stays up late at night; at the day's end, she's ready for bed, and she gets up in the morning eager to go the center. Her daughter expresses deep gratitude for the respite—she is now able to concentrate more on her children. And the idea of placing her mother in a nursing home is no longer mentioned.

Relatively new, day centers for the elderly are a growing trend. More than fifty such facilities already are functioning in twenty states. They are designed to serve the disabled and enfeebled who need constant attention, but not the around-the-clock care furnished by a hospital or a nursing home.

Besides the socializing and therapy, a major merit is that the center is much less costly than other forms of care. Going to a day center eliminates the need for and expense of a nurse-companion or a nursing home, both often more than a family can afford. At the Baltimore center, Mrs. Barrow's family pays only thirteen dollars a day, including transportation. A semiprivate room in a first-class nursing home would cost thirty to fifty dollars for a twenty-four-hour day.

Most day centers are still in a somewhat experimental stage. Generally, they observe criteria of the Department of Health, Education, and Welfare: a pleasant, safe environment; immediate access to skilled medical attention; provision for self-care training, including dressing and grooming; leisure-time activities in groups; supervised administration of required medication; and at least one nutritious meal a day.

The majority of centers are run in conjunction with hospitals or nursing homes supported by public or charitable funds. Increasing interest, however, has been shown by proprietary hospitals and nursing homes.

Unfortunately, Medicare does not cover charges

of such centers, and thus far, in most states, neither does Medicaid.

Getting Around

In many parts of the country, lack of transportation constitutes a major handicap for the elderly. If there is no way for them to move around, in or out of a community, healthy and physically mobile persons can be isolated as completely as if they were bedridden. Most older persons do not drive or own cars. Taxis are apt to be too costly, and fares for mass transit—where there are such facilities—keep rising.

For these reasons, many older adults can't enjoy free concerts or visits to parks. Supermarkets are often too far for walking, particularly with heavy packages. Some people, due to physical weakness—or because of fear in certain neighborhoods—need an escort. Without mobility, the elderly often abandon the idea of visiting friends, relatives, and senior centers, or engaging in other social activities.

Al Haven, seventy-two, has high blood pressure and a troubling hip condition. He could use free medical services, but finds traveling to the clinic very difficult. He would also like to go to church on Sundays, but that's three miles from his home. How can he get around?

His son learned that the local Red Cross had set up a transportation clearinghouse for the elderly, to provide door-to-door service when needed. Some community and voluntary organizations sponsor a special bus for needed trips. In Chicago, for example, the YMCA has set up a Senior Citizens Mobile Service. Transportation is free to such places as welfare agencies, and for outings or shopping tours.

Many who have taken advantage of the service have said they feel at least ten years younger as a result, and enduring friendships have been made during the rides.

In South Providence, Rhode Island, a station wagon bought by the State Division on Aging makes trips to doctors' offices and hospitals, though many people use it to go grocery shopping. Some senior citizen centers provide a bus that runs between members' homes and the centers. A "Dial-a-Bus" system in Menlo Park, California provides transportation for senior center members. The bus is also used for group outings.

As an alternative to regular bus transportation, a "Dial-a-Ride" project in Haddonfield, New Jersey provides door-to-door mobility. One bus is specially equipped for handicapped persons and people in wheelchairs. Wichita, Kansas has a similar system for low-income persons otherwise unable to get to medical facilities.

Elsewhere, particularly in suburban and rural areas, volunteers drive private cars for the elderly. North Carolina conducted a successful demonstration project, "Helping Wheels," in which one hundred volunteer senior drivers provided rides for their peers to club meetings, doctors, and churches.

Because over 40 percent of all older persons are poor or nearly poor, there is a great need for reduced fares on mass transit. More than fifty cities in fourteen states now offer senior citizens low fares on mass transit during nonrush hours. In San Francisco, senior citizens pay only five cents; New York City and Chicago charge half-fare; in Lorain, Ohio, it's free.

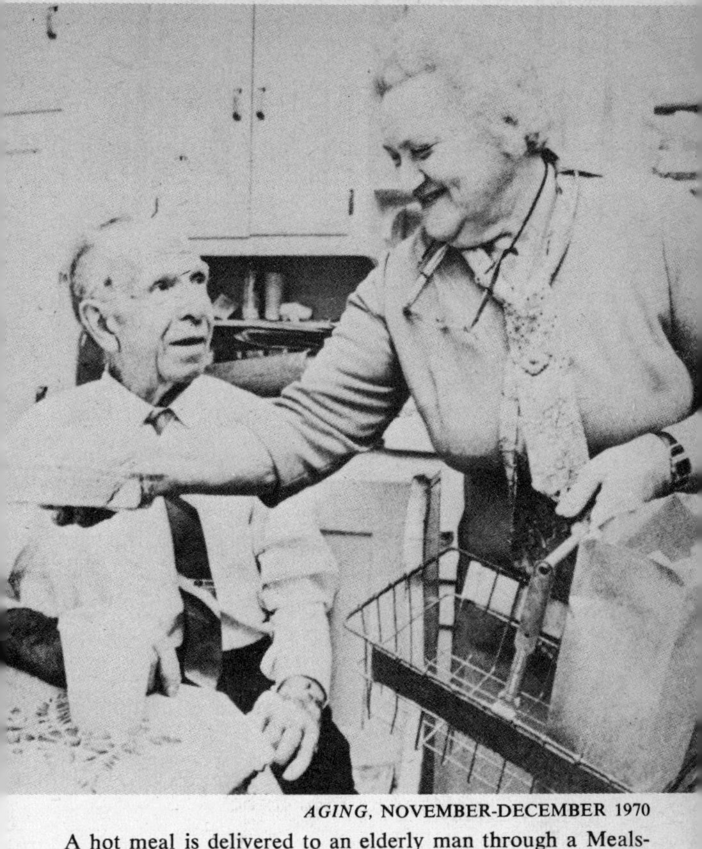

AGING, NOVEMBER-DECEMBER 1970

A hot meal is delivered to an elderly man through a Meals-on-Wheels program. One especially good feature of such programs is that they often provide an opportunity for retired persons in good health to work and to serve their peers at the same time.

More and better mobility gives the elderly a much needed lift in spirits, too. For people like Al Haven, getting around now has reopened the world.

Meal Services

"I eat alone, so it's hardly worth bothering to cook much," says Mary Oblonski, a painfully thin seventy-one-year-old. Mealtimes for her are irregular and too often she turns to snacks to satisfy her hunger. Her physician tells her she is undernourished, almost anemic. Mrs. Oblonski only shrugs helplessly.

Loneliness can lead to poor nutrition. Throughout Mrs. Oblonski's life, before her husband died and her children moved away, meals were a social occasion, a pleasant time for family gatherings. Deprived of the social element, meals hold little attraction for her.

For people living in solitude, or unable to market or prepare food satisfactorily for themselves, home-delivered, nutritious meals are available in many communities. Often they consist of a balanced hot noon meal and a cold supper left for the evening meal. This service, commonly known as "Meals on Wheels," may be carried on under the auspices of a religious or civic organization. In some communities, private cars are used to deliver the meals; in others, special vehicles with equipment to keep food hot or cold are used.

Charges vary, often based on ability to pay. Welfare departments may authorize and pay for the service to persons receiving old-age assistance or those with very low incomes. Meals on Wheels may also be purchased with food stamps.

One of the largest programs, in Baltimore, is run almost entirely by volunteers. It has ten separate kitchens, most located in churches, and uses the services of state nutritionists.

Another service is group meals in a social setting, which can be important for the mental well-being of older people. Dining locations are easily accessible, though food may be prepared elsewhere, such as in school cafeterias after the students' lunch hour. In St. Louis, eight to twelve neighborhood residents meet at one another's homes for a noon meal, which is delivered. Thus, old people can get together informally and eat family-style with a minimum of travel time. Denver has SAMS (Serve-A-Meal to Seniors) in five different locations. Rent and utilities are paid by host organizations such as the Salvation Army.

Many group-meal projects add programs featuring speakers on nutrition, health, Social Security, and other subjects of interest to the elderly. A number of senior clubs hold meetings in conjunction with a meal, then offer their recreational facilities. Besides better nutrition, group meals provide the fringe benefits of generating new friendships and a renewed interest in life. For the housebound, home-delivered meals provide a daily link with the outside world, someone to greet every day.

Aimed at aiding the isolated elderly, a $100-million nutritional program has been made available to all states through Title VII of the Older Americans Act. Projects funded under the program will provide hot meals at least five days a week for persons sixty or older. Though income will not be a criterion, priority will be given to low-income and minority people and "those who lack the skills to prepare nourishing meals, have limited mobility, or have feelings of rejection which obliterate the initiative necessary to prepare and eat a meal alone." Recipients may be required to pay all or part of the cost.

In-Home Care

Many elderly persons, even those who are chronically ill, want to remain in familiar surroundings—in their own apartments or homes—but they need regular, continuing assistance in personal care, housekeeping, laundry, or preparing meals. For these people, a homemaker-home health aide can be the difference between having to go into a nursing home or living independently. Even when an older adult does not live alone, this kind of help can lessen the stress on the whole family.

Typically, a homemaker-home health aide is a mature woman who is skilled in home management and who has an understanding of human behavior. She has had some basic training, including personal and household care, but she is not a pinch hitter for a nurse or for a maid. She is supervised by a registered nurse, a social worker, or other professional as part of a health or social service team. When she functions under the supervision of a nurse, she may perform a variety of out-of-hospital services.

In many communities, there are homemaker-home health aide agencies. In others, homemaker-home health aide service is coordinated or operated by a multiservice social agency, a welfare department, or a visiting-nurse association. In all, about two thousand agencies throughout the country provide homemaker-home health aide service, but this is not nearly enough to meet the need.

Licensed practical nurses for skilled practical nursing in the home can be hired through agencies in this field. For people who need a registered nurse, on an occasional or regular basis, 520 nonprofit Visiting Nurse Associations are located in cities and towns all over the country. The fee per visit varies from community to community and covers costs to the association. Nationwide, the median charge is $10.40. In New York City, the charge is $20.00 a visit, but it is adjustable to what the patient can afford. In emergencies, of course, the nearest hospital should be called.

About twenty-three hundred home-health agencies are qualified under the Medicare program. Some provide homemaker-home health aides; others do not, but do offer the services of registered nurses, physiotherapists, or other personnel. Medicare reimburses for home-health services under both Part A and Part B. After a minimum of three days in a hospital or after a discharge from an extended-care facility, Part A pays for up to one hundred hospital-related home-health visits within a twelve-month period. Part B pays the home-care agency for up to one hundred home health-care visits each year when a patient has no prior hospital stay, if such services are provided according to a treatment plan approved by a physician.

Many communities have created other ways to help the elderly care for themselves at home. In Washington State's STEP (Service to Elderly People) program, teenagers do heavy housework, mow lawns, help with other chores. Elder-Care in Jasper, Alabama provides housecleaning, marketing, and house repairs done by older persons employed by the local Community Action Agency.

Friendly Visitors

Joe Zimmerman, seventy-five, a retired cutter in the garment industry, was often depressed, still grief-stricken after the death of his wife. "I'm just put away on the shelf," he'd say. Recently, his morale was raised by a Friendly Visitor from his trade union, sixty-six-year-old Sam Berger, who had also been a cutter. Mr. Berger came to sit with him one morning, chatted about many things, later arranged for occasional household help, took Mr. Zimmerman for a hearing test and to be fitted for a hearing aid. "I feel like a human being again," says Mr. Zimmerman.

Friendly visiting is organized neighborliness. Once a week, or more often, volunteers or paid workers call on homebound older persons. To those who have few friends or relatives, the visitors bring continuing companionship. They may play cards or chess, lend an arm to lean on during a shopping trip, or write letters for the older person. Or the two may just sit and talk for a while.

In a recent survey of elderly people in Portland, Oregon, home visits to shut-ins and live-alones topped the list of needs—even ahead of the need for higher income. In Portland, "home visits" include some household chores and handyman-type services as well as friendly meetings.

The visitors may be social workers or volunteers. Their major essential qualities: a genuine capacity for friendliness and reliability in sticking to a regular schedule. In one western community, a school bus driver visits several old folk every day between the time he delivers the children and the time he picks them up again. In several cities, high-school students do the visiting, run errands, mostly talk with their "adopted grandparents."

Certain trade unions have launched impressive Friendly Visitor projects for their retired members. Most outstanding is the one conducted by the International Ladies' Garment Workers Union in New York. Of the staff of ninety, over seventy visitors are themselves retired workers aged sixty-four to eighty-four. Besides former operators, cutters, finishers, and office clerks, the ILGWU sometimes hires retired bakers, furriers, and postmen for the program. Each year, they call on twenty-eight thousand retirees. They give information on health and social services; assist in filing for Medicaid, Medicare, public housing; escort people to and from doctors and hospitals. The ILGWU project is considered a national model for such programs.

The elderly find the Friendly Visitors a real boon. Some typical comments: "I look forward to her visits." . . . "It makes me feel like I'm still somebody worth talking to." . . . "It gives me a chance to speak of things in my heart."

Telephone Reassurance

Ella Berns, a spry seventy-two-year-old, prefers to live in her own studio apartment. Her one fear is that some day she might fall, "maybe break a hip," or become suddenly ill and be unable to reach her phone to call for help. Recently, she read a news item about a woman who died that way.

For just such contingencies, many communities now have telephone reassurance projects. Calls are made to older persons who have few, if any, outside contacts for long periods of time. The calls come each day at a predetermined time. If there's no answer, a personal check is made immediately, usually through a neighbor, relative, or nearby police or fire station. Such details are decided before the service is started.

Fortunately, Ella Berns took on the service. One day, some months later, her regular caller noticed a slurring in her speech, though Miss Berns had no complaint. When a check of her condition revealed she had suffered a heart spasm, she was rushed to a hospital in time for proper treatment.

Telephone reassurance becomes a lifeline for live-alones. Various organizations and agencies sponsor the services. Callers may be other elderly people, or they may be teenagers. In Florida, daily calls are made by senior center members; in Albuquerque, by a hospital auxiliary and the Business and Professional Women's Club; in Ohio, six churches cooperate as sponsors. Boston's Family Service Association has "Lifeline," through which "captains" call sixty-five elderly persons every day.

Another type of phone service is known as "Dial-a-Listener." The older person is given a number to call if he or she just wants to talk. In Davenport, Iowa, elderly professional people are the listeners. In New York, the Red Cross runs a Telephone Club for homebound and lonely people.

Open Doors to Culture

Libraries and museums are excellent resources for leisure-time activities for older adults. Public library extension services are designed for people who can't conveniently use the regular facilities. These services may include delivery of books and materials to homebound older persons, either through bookmobiles or personal distribution by aides. Subbranches are often located in senior citizen centers and in residences for older people.

In Milwaukee, all the paid library aides in the city's "Over Sixty" service are themselves sixty-five-plus. And in Vermont, where older persons were hired to amplify their meager incomes by working as temporary senior aides in small libraries, they proved so valuable that a number were retained on a permanent basis.

Some libraries sponsor programs specifically for the aging. Among the exemplary programs, Boston's "Never Too Late Groups" function at the main library and at fourteen branches. Cleveland has sponsored the "Live Long and Like It Library Club," which conducts meetings on such topics as current affairs and biographies. The Wake County Library in Raleigh, North Carolina cosponsors courses on basic living skills and the rights of, and benefits available to, older adults.

Elsewhere, group programs conducted or sponsored by libraries, either at their buildings or at outside locations, include clubs for the elderly, discussion groups, and adult education courses.

Not widely enough known is the fact that many libraries have large-print and talking books for those with failing vision or physical disability. In Baltimore, staff members of the Pratt Library make regular visits to recipients of talking books to demonstrate how to use the equipment and to help select materials.

In addition, a number of libraries have recordings, tapes and cassettes, magnifying equipment, page turners, and projectors. And libraries usually publish lists of local activities at least once a month; so a library card opens many doors.

With funding by the Administration on Aging, the

Kennedy Center for the Performing Arts and the National Council on the Aging are involved in a national effort to increase opportunities for older Americans to both enjoy and participate in the performing and visual arts.

Museums are also likely to offer special programs. And the elderly can take advantage of free concerts and film showings—often listed in the local press—as well as adult courses at local high schools or community colleges.

Opportunities to Serve or Work

Gertrude Myers, physically fit and fully alert at sixty-eight, felt restless and useless just sitting home, watching television, playing solitaire. At a neighbor's suggestion, she joined SERVE (Serve and Enrich Retirement by Volunteer Experience), conducted by the Community Service Society in New York City. Her assignment: to work with a mentally retarded boy at the Willowbrook State School.

There, for the past two years, Mrs. Myers has been playing and talking with Timmy, giving him her love. At first, he wouldn't speak, lay all day on his back in bed. Now he not only sits up but goes for rides as Mrs. Myers pushes his wheelchair, and he even walks. Recently, Timmy has begun to play with other children.

In most communities, all kinds of opportunities are available for volunteer and even paid work for those who can get around. Valuable skills and experience need not be wasted; many older people prove to be dependable, capable, willing workers.

Nationally, there are three major service programs predominantly for older adults: the Foster Grandparents Program, Retired Senior Volunteer Program (RSVP), and Service … utives (SCORE)—all funded b… agency.

In the landmark Foster Grand… low-income people over sixty work p… children in infant homes, convalescen… schools for the disturbed or retarded. "Gran… do not replace regular staff, but establish a p…son-to-person relationship with a child. They receive an hourly stipend; and they receive the child's affection and trust.

RSVP offers opportunities for voluntary community service in schools, courts, libraries, museums, hospitals, nursing homes, and programs for the homebound.

Of course, virtually every community has openings for volunteers. There are, for instance, the Green Thumb and Green Light projects, which employ low-income men and women in rural areas to beautify parks, roadside, and other public areas. Some of the most effective volunteer programs have set up talent pools.

For those who want to supplement inadequate incomes, the Senior Worker Action Program (SWAP), under the auspices of the Office of Economic Opportunity, promotes employment—particularly part-time and temporary jobs—among older people. The program is usually housed in a community or neighborhood center. Staff members attempt to find and recruit older workers, interview and counsel applicants, develop new placements. Jobs run the gamut from school aides to babysitters, companions, handymen, homemakers, and seamstresses.

Many older people are being trained in new skills or helped to brush up unused skills, such as typing.

…del Cities areas, elderly residents are …ed in children's day care centers, thus per…ing parents to take jobs. The National Council of Senior Citizens employs men and women part time in twenty-one projects from coast to coast, performing services that include low-cost meal preparation and outreach activities.

Schools are recruiting older people to give children educational enrichment. Dade County, Florida public schools, for example, hired people over fifty-five as teacher aides in industrial arts and language arts classes. These aides make it possible for regular teachers to handle twice as many pupils. In Vermont, senior library aides enable public libraries to remain open longer and on more days. Senior citizens in two Michigan counties work as tourist guides at fishing and camping sites.

Private industry, too, is dipping into the older-people reservoir. One company hires former employees to guide visiting salesmen through its plants. Mature Temps, the free employment service of the American Association of Retired Persons, has offices in at least thirteen major cities and places older people in temporary paid jobs. One New York firm hires fifty Mature Temps every month. A group of retirees in Norwalk, Connecticut has organized the Senior Personnel Placement Bureau, and similar groups are springing up elsewhere.

Senior Home Craftsmen in Maryland are men who do minor home repairs such as replacing faucet washers and fixing leaks. At Good Neighbor Family Aides, elderly women who have been homemakers offer aid to other older persons or to families that need help in caring for elderly relatives. These women receive training in home nursing at the local

Red Cross chapter and in home economics state university extension agent.

Senior Centers

Unquestionably, the most widespread socializing and recreational resource for older people are the familiar Senior Citizens Centers, which are playing an increasingly central role in the lives of old people. They may go by other names: "Golden Age Club," "Silver Age," "Over Sixty," or "Sixty-five Plus."

Here, elderly persons come together for diverse programs and "fun and games." Activities range from card-playing to professionally directed hobby and group ventures, stimulating lectures, and just chit-chat. Some centers provide counseling and referral services, as well as a job registry. Others act as central umbrella agencies for virtually everything related to the elderly. A number offer hot midday meals, either free or at a nominal charge.

Some centers are run rather informally, while others reflect a highly structured approach in terms of staff and facilities. At one popular hobby-oriented center, men and women are found sewing, painting, working at ceramics and photography, attending exercise classes. Here, outings are arranged each summer, and members go in groups to theaters and museums. An Oklahoma City center gives courses in archeology, creative writing, piano, whatever the members ask for.

Nashville, Tennessee has a highly comprehensive program, boasting a main senior center with twelve satellite centers. They offer special health education programs—glaucoma screenings, classes for diabetics, courses for people with hearing loss.

More than twelve hundred centers are now open

throughout the country, and they may be found in every state. Of the main categories, a Multipurpose Center operates in a permanent place and is open year-round at least four hours a day, five days a week, with a professional staff. A Senior Citizens Center may not have a professional staff or a full scope of programs. A Senior Citizen Club usually meets fewer than three days a week, and may not have a permanent location or paid leaders. Many public housing projects reserve space for senior centers. In one Colorado town, a former railroad station has been converted into a senior center.

Membership is usually free, though certain centers charge a small fee, perhaps fifty cents a month; the fee at Golden Age Clubs may be a few dollars a year.

Legal Assistance

In their later years, especially if they have to get along on a low income, people may run into all sorts of legal problems.

John Gordin, seventy-three, was having trouble with his landlord, who refused to make needed repairs. His downstairs neighbor, Simeon Brown, a sixty-five-year-old retired electrician who suffered from arthritis, was inexplicably denied Medicare coverage. Neither knew where to seek advice, and both were reluctant to get involved with anything "legal."

They could have gone to the local office of the Legal Aid Society. Throughout the nation, over 750 legal assistance offices are open to people like John Gordin and Simeon Brown. Services are based on financial eligibility. Typically, there is no fee; where one is charged, it is nominal. In some programs, however, clients are required to help defray actual out-of-pocket filing fees and miscellaneous court costs for certain cases.

The elderly face much the same legal concerns as others in the population, with some extras thrown in: Social Security or pension claims, welfare rights, Medicare and Medicaid benefits, eligibility for special housing; also problems related to probate and estate planning, making a will, taxes, disability insurance, driver's license, apartment leases, credit arrangements, consumer contracts.

In one case, a blind man living solely on Social Security sought assistance from Boston's Council of Elders. With the help of a legal aide, he was certified under Aid to the Blind and received $4,600 in back payments. Another elderly man, a welfare recipient, had been denied a request for false teeth; a legal aide obtained the money for him on the ground that lack of them would harm his health and force him into a nursing home.

Alternatives to the Legal Aid Society are the local bar association or lawyers' reference service.

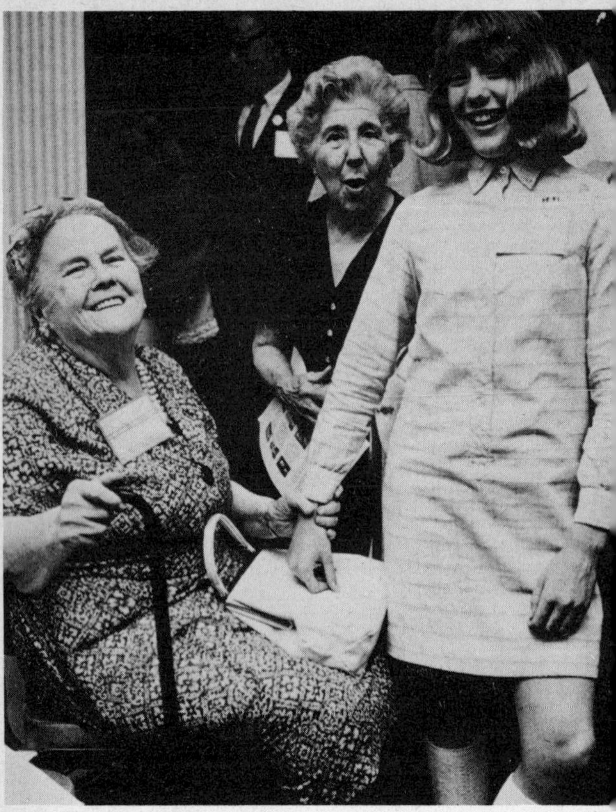

AGING, JULY 1968

These are delegates at a National Council of Senior Citizens convention. This council and similar organizations are helping senior citizens to gain a stronger voice in America.

13

The Seniors Come of Age

by MARY LEONARD

As this article indicates, gray power is a phenomenon on the rise. The bill mentioned below that would create an Illinois Department of Services for the Aging was signed into law in August 1973. As seniors become more organized and through a declining birthrate come to constitute a larger percentage of the population, their power should increase dramatically. If it does, will attitudes toward the elderly become more favorable, or will gray power cause resentment among some as black power did?

BECAUSE people like Mary Herrick, age seventy-eight, Marie Keeler, age eighty-two, and Major Roy Nordheimer, age eighty-five, refused to retire to their rocking chairs and "refused to die" when they

"The Seniors Come of Age," by Mary Leonard, from *Chicago Today*, August 7, 1973. Reprinted by permission of *Chicago Today*.

reached their sixty-fifth birthdays, thousands of senior citizens in Illinois today are playing politics rather than pinochle.

Call it senior power, they'll call it a matter of dignity; it's a fact that in just the last few years, vocal, activist senior citizens like Miss Herrick, Mrs. Keeler, and Major Nordheimer have been rising up angry against the typical old-folks stereotype and have been demanding attention and equality in the system that, they say, tended to reject them when they reached the arbitrary "old age" of sixty-five.

Now, their hoarse throats from protests and their writer's cramp from correspondence to Springfield [the state capital] are being revenged. The CTA [Chicago Transit Authority] has instituted twenty-four-hour reduced fares for seniors, the state is offering a maximum $500 property tax rebate to those over sixty-five who meet certain qualifications, and, in what could be an important victory, a bill to establish a state Department of Services for the Aging has passed both houses of the legislature and awaits Governor Walker's signature.

"While it's not a cure-all, this agency, to coordinate services for the aging and to be directed by a senior citizen, would be a great step," says Major Nordheimer, the former president of the Chicago Area Council of Senior Citizen Organizations, today some fifteen thousand members strong. "For the first time, senior citizens would be accountable for their own destinies. If it works, Illinois' action will be a lighthouse for other states to follow."

If the bill, forwarded by Lieutenant-Governor Neil Hartigan, does not become the victim of a political power play on the governor's part, that "lighthouse" will also stand as a monument to the hard work and organizational skills of activist seniors who made it their business to replace afternoons in the park with afternoons in Springfield's hearing rooms.

"The establishment of this office is the direct result of activities on the part of senior citizens who testified in Springfield or wrote letters to the legislators," Major Nordheimer says. "Back in 1967, we'd go to representatives on bended knees, asking them to help us. Today, the politicians are coming to us, asking us if we approve of this or that."

Whether it has been through groups like Nordheimer's Chicago Area Council; Miss Herrick's class in the Loop College in Civil Rights for Senior Citizens; Mrs. Keeler's efforts to organize Uptown, the Chicago community with the largest concentration of senior citizens; or Lou Jungheim's senior citizen coalition in the Citizens' Action Program (CAP), the politics of protest, if not confrontation, has been working.

At least they're begining to get the message across: that there are more than one million persons over age sixty-five in Illinois, with more than six hundred thousand of them in the Chicago area; that one out of every six elderly persons has an income below the poverty line, defined as $2,100 by the Social Security Administration; that as the cost of living skyrockets, most senior citizens get by on a fixed income of Social Security and pension benefits. In 1972, Social Security retirement benefits averaged out at $1,938 a year.

Coupled with these statistics are the facts that there are some twenty thousand elderly persons on waiting lists for low-income housing—who may wait as long as five years for accommodation; that health systems aren't delivering their services to the aging; that drug costs are prohibitive; that police protection is what seniors consider "inadequate," especially on Social Security check delivery days; that the elderly are discriminated against in employment and loan opportunities; that federal social service cutbacks threaten to erase substantial Medicare benefits and programs for the homebound.

But perhaps even more damaging than the physical problems, senior citizens confess, are the psychological ones.

"While only 4 percent of all senior citizens are in institutions, society has a pattern of treating all of us as senile," says Miss Herrick, a teacher in Chicago for thirty-eight years. "Because we know that we possess a wealth of useful experience, competent old people resent being treated as children and looked down upon. Old people want to be counted in; they're becoming more and more indignant of a stereotype that pushes them into a corner."

"We find a peculiar attitude: if you go to the butcher, you pay a top price for aged meat; if you go the liquor store, you're looking for the oldest wine or oldest whisky," Major Nordheimer adds. "When it comes to old human beings, however, they're down at the bottom of the totem pole and get no consideration at all."

And though their tactics run the gamut from letter-writing to out-and-out confrontation, the seniors, like other minority groups, have found that to get consideration requires more than passive acceptance of the status quo.

"Senior citizens are beginning to realize that if you don't speak up, you won't be heard. We have to fight for what we want; things don't come on a silver platter," says Lou Jungheim, cochairman of CAP's senior citizen coalition. "To accomplish what's necessary, we have to get on our hind legs and make people realize we're not has-beens."

To bring home that point, CAP seniors, who represent about 160 organizations and are characterized by Mr. Jungheim as "a bunch of radicals," are dealing in direct actions and person-to-person confrontations.

Their current target is AT&T, from whom they hope to win half-price telephone rates for seniors.

To get what they want, these seniors have gone as high as the Manhattan suite of AT&T's chairman, they have staged demonstrations in Bell Telephone's Chicago office, and they have sent busloads of people to Springfield to lobby against phone-rate increases.

Miss Herrick, whose class in civil rights for senior citizens meets once a week to discuss everything from inflation to crime to euthanasia, takes—initially—a less radical approach to winning recognition for senior citizens.

"To me, the picket line is the place to go when nothing else works. I'm afraid we would lose support through confrontation, and we are better off working through the system," Miss Herrick says. "Confrontation is not the best way if we can do it another way—though I'm not sure we won't eventually reach that point."

Nor have the seniors in Chicago reached the point of forming their own local chapter of the Gray Panthers, a Philadelphia-based action group of old and young people aligned to fight age discrimination.

"If it's just going to be one more group, just another group with the same people working under a different name, we really don't need it here," Miss Herrick says. "More than new groups, we need leaders with charisma and programs to meet the needs of the people and their community, programs to keep the older people interested and active."

At eighty-two, Marie Keeler is one charismatic leader in the Uptown community, where some thirty thousand Chicago senior citizens make their home. Under the banner of the Uptown Senior Citizens Council, this group is aiming to organize the community, reach out to isolated elderly people, and solve some of the health, housing, income, and crime problems there.

"This is senior power—not wearing buttons, but actually generating power by doing something in a united way," Major Nordheimer says. "Look at Niagara Falls, the greatest generator of power in the world—just many tiny, individual drops, all going in the same direction."

"Senior citizens don't want escape mechanisms, they don't necessarily want recreation programs; they want to find things to help themselves, and they want to find ways to help others," Miss Herrick adds. "More than anything, they're trying to make sense of the world they live in and do something about it while they still can."

14

Selected Poems

The poems here offer three poets' perspectives on old age. Although not all are of the same literary quality, each selection rings true. The first is by one of America's most distinguished poets, the second by a minor turn-of-the-century American poet, and the third by a seventy-four-year-old Monroe, Michigan man who prior to 1973 had never published a poem.

Provide, Provide

The witch that came (thc withered hag)
To wash the steps with pail and rag
Was once the beauty Abishag,

The picture pride of Hollywood.
Too many fall from great and good
For you to doubt the likelihood.

Die early and avoid the fate.
Or if predestined to die late,
Make up your mind to dic in state.

Make the whole stock exchange your own!
If need be occupy a throne,
Where nobody can call *you* crone.

Some have relied on what they knew,
Others on being simply true.
What worked for them might work for you.

No memory of having starred
Atones for later disregard
Or keeps the end from being hard.

Better to go down dignified
With boughten friendship at your side
Than none at all. Provide, provide!

ROBERT FROST

HARPER'S WEEKLY, JULY 13, 1867

These two women whiling away time in a nineteenth-century old ladies' home in Brooklyn, New York do not seem too badly off. But the impoverished old a century ago were generally as reluctant to be institutionalized as the elderly are today.

Over the Hill to the Poor-House

Over the hill to the poor-house I'm trudgin' my
weary way,—
I, a woman of seventy, and only a trifle gray,—
I, who am smart and chipper, for all the years I've
told,
As many another woman that's only half as old.

Over the hill to the poor-house,—I can't quite make
it clear!
Over the hill to the poor-house,—it seems so horrid
queer!
Many a step I've taken a-toilin' to and fro,
But this is a sort of journey I never thought to go.

What is the use of heapin' on me a pauper's shame?
Am I lazy or crazy? am I blind or lame?
True, I am not so supple, nor yet so awful stout;
But charity ain't no favor, if one can live without.

I am willin' and anxious an' ready any day
To work for a decent livin', and pay my honest way;
For I can earn my victuals, an' more too, I'll
be bound,
If anybody only is willin' to have me around.

Once I was young and handsome,—I was, upon
my soul,—
Once my cheeks were roses, my eyes as black as coal;
And I can't remember, in them days, of hearin'
people say,
For any kind of a reason, that I was in their way.

'Taint no use of boastin', or talkin' over free,
But many a house an' home was open then to me;
Many a han'some offer I had from likely men,
And nobody ever hinted that I was a burden then.

And when to John I was married, sure he was good
and smart,
But he and all the neighbors would own I done
my part;
For life was all before me, an' I was young an'
strong,
And I worked the best that I could in tryin' to get
along.

And so we worked together; and life was hard,
but gay,
With now and then a baby for to cheer us on our
way;

Till we had half a dozen, an' all growed clean an' neat,
All went to school like others, an' had enough to eat.

So we worked for the childr'n, and raised 'em every one;
Worked for 'em summer and winter, just as we ought to've done;
Only perhaps we humored 'em, which some good folks condemn,
But every couple's childr'n's a heap the best to them.

Strange how much we think of our blessed little ones!—
I'd have died for my daughters, I'd have died for my sons;
And God He made that rule of love; but when we're old and gray,
I've noticed it sometimes somehow fails to work the other way.

Strange, another thing; when our boys and girls was grown,
And when, exceptin' Charley, they'd left us there alone;
When John he nearer an' nearer come, and dearer seemed to be,
The Lord of Hosts He come one day an' took him away from me.

Still I was bound to struggle, an' never to cringe or fall,—
Still I worked for Charley, for Charley was now my all;
And Charley was pretty good to me, with scarce a word or frown,

Till at last he went a-courtin', and brought a wife
from town.

She was somewhat dressy, an' hadn't a pleasant
smile,—
She was quite conceity, and carried a heap o' style;
But if ever I tried to be friends, I did with her,
I know;
But she was hard and proud, an' I couldn't make
it go.

She had an edication, an' that was good for her;
But when she twitted me on mine, 'twas carryin'
things too fur;
An' I told her once, 'fore company (an' it almost
made her sick),
That I never swallowed a grammar, or 'et a
'rithmetic.

So 'twas only a few days before the thing was done,—
They was a family of themselves, and I another one;
And a very little cottage one family will do,
But I never have seen a house that was big enough
for two.

An' I never could speak to suit her, never could
please her eye,
An' it made me independent, an' then I didn't try;
But I was terribly staggered, an' felt it like a blow,
When Charley turned ag'in me, an' told me I could
go.

I went to live with Susan, but Susan's house was
small,
And she was always a-hintin' how snug it was for
us all;

And what with her husband's sisters, and what with
childr'n three,
'Twas easy to discover that there wasn't room for me.

An' then I went to Thomas, the oldest son I've got,
For Thomas's buildings'd cover the half of an acre
lot;
But all the childr'n was on me—I couldn't stand
their sauce—
And Thomas said I needn't think I was comin' there
to boss.

An' then I wrote to Rebecca, my girl who lives out
West,
And to Isaac, not far from her—some twenty miles
at best;
And one of 'em said 'twas too warm there for any
one so old,
And t'other had an opinion the climate was too cold.

So they have shirked and slighted me, an' shifted
me about—
So they have well-nigh soured me, an' wore my old
heart out;
But still I've borne up pretty well, an' wasn't much
put down,
Till Charley went to the poor-master, an' put me on
the town.

Over the hill to the poor-house—my childr'n dear,
goodbye!
Many a night I've watched you when only God was
nigh;
And God'll judge between us; but I will al'ays pray
That you shall never suffer the half I do to-day.

WILL M. CARLETON

Retired or Tired

I am a retired man
  I loaf around all day
A doing little odds and ends
  I'm in my dear wife's way.

I try to keep out from under foot,
  But what can an old man do
That's hard of hearing, stiff of legs,
  And aches all over too?

I'll just have to do my best
  To keep a cheerful mind.
Help my wife, do what I can
  To keep her feeling fine.

GEORGE VROOMAN

From *Reflections: A Literary and Fine Arts Magazine by the Senior Adults of Monroe County, Michigan,* vol. I, 1974. Reprinted by permission.

15

"Bonus Notches, Pal"

by DOROTHY WALWORTH

This final selection tells the story of a happy elderly couple with many friends and a loving son. It serves as a reminder that, despite the difficulties that many older Americans face, friends, children, or a zest for life like that displayed by the husband in this piece can help to make the later years enjoyable.

WE SAW HIM by the gangplank when the stewards were shouting, "All ashore that's going ashore!" He was a sturdy old man, wrinkled as a walnut, wearing a new-looking tweed topcoat. Standing by him was his tiny raisin of a wife. Her veil kept catching on her spectacles. Her corsage of red roses was withering in the winter cold.

"'Bonus Notches, Pal'," by Dorothy Walworth, from *Reader's Digest*, March 1948. Copyright 1948 by The Reader's Digest Association, Inc. Reprinted by permission.

JOHN McENROE

Many elderly parents continue to be involved in the lives of their grown children and derive considerable satisfaction from this.

Few friends had braved the freezing New York weather to see any passenger off. Yet this couple was surrounded by a chattering, laughing crowd, shabby men with red faces, women whose clothes showed signs of long use. They said they just wished they could take a swell trip to South America like Ed and Marge.

The whistle blew. The friends of Ed and Marge called from the dock, "Remember us to the boy!" Marge began to cry, her veil and spectacles a hopeless tangle. "Come now, Mother," Ed boomed. "Ain't you proud?" And she said, "I wish they could all be lucky like us."

Ours was not a cruise boat. It carried freight and about forty passengers, North and South Americans, to Panama, Ecuador, and Peru. To these passengers, most of them traveling on business, an ocean voyage was no novelty. They had a tired, wary look, which meant they were not going to get involved in shipboard friendships. To such a crowd, Ed and Marge did not seem to belong.

After dinner, my husband and I circled the deck, exchanging greetings in guarded fashion. Whenever we passed South Americans, we said, *"Buenas noches,"* hoping we had the correct accent. But Ed did not worry about his accent. He bellowed with confident, neighborly good humor, "Bonus Notches."

Next morning, when we stepped out on the deck, the air had turned warmer. Under a soft sky, the sea was smooth with wide white ruffles. Ed was talking to a seaman with a mop and pail. When we approached, he thumped my husband on the back with a fist like a pine knot.

"Look at that there sun!" he said, pointing to a red blaze in the east. "I got up extra early so's I wouldn't miss my first sunup at sea. Mother and me never been on a boat before. Matter of fact, we ain't been anywheres but New Jersey.

"Did you see our neighbors on the dock?" he continued. "They all got little farms in South Jersey, just like us. Icy roads and all, they come most a hundred miles to see us off. Mother and me got to New York a week ago. Put up at the Waldorf-Astoria Hotel. What with all the fuss and feathers, Mother's real tired. But she wouldn't want to miss that sun. I'll fetch her. Bonus Notches, pal." It didn't matter to him that *"Buenas noches"* was a greeting used in the evening.

By the end of the first day, everyone called him "Bonus Notches." To everyone, he talked about things that the worldly-wise took for granted: the steward bringing Mother and him their breakfast.

What solid comfort! The white napkins. The little lights over the beds, so handy to switch off and on.

My husband and I succumbed at once to his warmth. But his loud voice, his lack of grammar, his naïve assumption that we were all friends annoyed many passengers.

"Wouldn't you know it?" mourned a North American woman who shared our table in the dining room. "We put forth every effort to show South Americans that we are not a nation of roughnecks. And now here is this creature running around the boat, talking about a suite at the Waldorf-Astoria. He's just the type of vulgar tourist who makes a wreck of our Good Neighbor policy. I'm glad I speak Spanish so I can tell all the Latin Americans on board, 'Please don't judge our country by a man like that!' "

"I would be quite willing to have South Americans judge our country by Bonus Notches," my husband said firmly. "He is the type of man one still finds all over America, thank God. In the pastures of New England, the wheat fields of Nebraska, the timberland of the Far West. He has all the virtues that built our country, including the old American trait of being free of pretense."

The third morning out, we had all gathered on the wide sun deck, leaning back in our chairs in well-bred silence. When the steward brought our eleven o'clock bouillon, Bonus Notches joined us, but did not take a cup. Instead, he stood with legs spread wide, fists thrust deep into his pockets, looking at us for what seemed like a long time.

"Listen, pals," he said. "There's something I got to get off my chest. I don't want to be going around here with you good folks thinking I'm somebody I ain't. To put it all in a nutshell, Mother and me

SUZANNE OPTON

Satisfaction and creative fulfillment in old age are not reserved just for such famous people as Robert Frost, Grandma Moses, and Frank Lloyd Wright—obscure individuals like this elderly man, shown playing the organ in his home, can enjoy these rewards too.

could never of afforded this trip, not in a million years. It's our boy who's gave it to us."

There was a small silence. Then Bonus Notches continued with eager pride: "Mother and me had two boys. We put the oldest one, Tom, through college, because I've always admired an education. The youngest never got a chance to go. He was killed at Iwo Jima.

"Of course, Tom really ain't a boy. He's a man, turning thirty-five. For ten years he's been down in Peru with an oil company, hundreds of miles up in them Andes Mountains. Now he's getting pretty good pay. We ain't seen him in all this while.

"Right after the war, Tom wrote he was planning to surprise us with something special. First thing we knew, tickets come in the mail, and reservations at the Waldorf-Astoria Hotel, and money for new clothes, and a letter saying, 'I got to travel by muleback, by train, and by plane, but I'll be on the dock at Callao to meet you.' Well, I just thought I'd tell you, so's you wouldn't think Mother and me was big shots."

Everyone spoke at once, assuring Bonus Notches he had a right to be very pleased. The South Americans who understood English translated what he had said to their friends. We all exchanged understanding smiles. It seemed just then that we, citizens of a dozen countries on two continents, all belonged to one country: the nation of fathers and mothers. We held a single simple creed: our children. We shared a common destiny—to love, and hope we were loved in return, and never, in our heart of hearts, to be quite sure.

There was no one, after that, who said that Bonus Notches was crude. All of us felt that in him we were seeing the reassuring glow of a fine old-fashioned story, where ordinary things are changed to gold, and everyone lives happily ever after. We experienced heartfelt joy in this simple tale of a son who remembered his father and mother, not counting the cost, but lavishly, in full measure running over.

We never saw much of Mother. Bonus Notches told us she was down in the cabin, writing letters. She had dozens of friends who wanted to know what it was like to be on the ocean. "Friends have always meant a lot to Mother," he said.

One afternoon, however, when the teacart was making its round, Mother joined us in the lounge.

"Seems so good to eat something I haven't cooked," she said. "I'm going to make the most of it while I can. Ed says he's told you about Tom. I reckon he didn't tell you why Tom feels so special about his dad. You see, when Tom was ready for college, our farm was doing poorly. Some folks said Tom should stay home and help his father. But Ed had always fancied schooling, so Tom went to Yale. He worked his way through, best as he could, but there still was extra expenses. So Ed hired out nights as a carpenter.

"Tom said, when he first went to Peru, that as soon as he could he would bring us down there like a king and a queen. I didn't think I'd live to see the day. This is all like a dream. Dad and me ain't real old, but we figure this is the last time we'll see Tom."

"Surely not," I said. "Perhaps you could all live in Peru together."

"That's what Tom told us. But now that he's a grown man, there's just one thing we can do for him—we can leave him free. So we'll visit him a couple of months and then go back to the farm."

When we reached the West Indies, we told Bonus Notches the names of the islands we were passing. How pleased he was when we showed him San Salvador, where Columbus first landed. "That guy deserves a lot of credit," he said. Then he earnestly wrung the hand of every Spaniard on board and bellowed, "Congratulations, pal!"

We anchored off Cristobal, in sight of the Panama Canal, at four o'clock in the morning. My husband went on deck so as to tell Bonus Notches some facts about this region. But he returned in a quarter of an hour. "That man knows more than I do already," he said. "He and the Ambassador spent most of the night on the top deck, talking their heads off. He was telling me just how the locks work."

As we crept through the canal, Bonus Notches stood at the rail all day, even going without his lunch so as not to miss a thing.

"My, what a pile of planning it must of took to dig this thing and make it come out even with no water left over," he said. "I tell you, the United States is a great country. Always thought so, but now I'm surer than ever."

Since Bonus Notches had congratulated the Spaniards on Columbus, they now returned the compliment by congratulating him on the canal. He accepted their felicitations in a dignified manner, with a simple "Thanks, pal."

Having reached the Pacific, Bonus Notches surrendered himself to the expectation of wonders. So, for him, wonders appeared everywhere. If any bit of spray splashed high, he said it was a whale spouting. Moreover, he frequently discovered devilfish and sharks with double sets of teeth, swimming just below the surface of the water. Even an eminent naturalist on board, often called to the rail by the astonishment of Bonus Notches, never denied seeing any of these things.

We were anchored for two days off the steaming coast of Ecuador, loading bananas. The great green bunches were brought on board by blacks in pink and yellow loincloths and bright earrings. While the rest of us gasped in the heat, Bonus Notches went down into the hold to watch the loading. We saw him eating sandwiches on one of the banana barges alongside. He returned with a dozen friendships he had struck up among the banana carriers, who, he said, were fine fellows. We asked him how he could tell, since he did not know a word of their language.

"Why, one of them fellows give me his earrings," he said. "Wouldn't take a penny for them neither. We was just setting there on the barge, passing the time of day—I mean, I was smiling friendly at him, and he was smiling at me. All of a sudden, he ups with the earrings. Reckon I'll never know why he done it."

Our boat passed the northern tip of Peru. We said it was a pity the voyage would be over so soon, when, on account of Bonus Notches, we had all become such close friends. Even those of us who did not understand each other's language were getting on famously with smiles and broken phrases in Spanish and English. We found each other, as Bonus Notches had found the banana carrier, fine fellows.

We knew that once we came to shore we would again be wary and worldly wise. But, here and now, we believed it was good for human beings not to keep to themselves, but to become involved with their fellow men. We shared, under that blue cup of sky, Bonus Notches' faith in the future. The world might grow better, we said, and men be brothers.

The day before we reached Callao, we were suddenly afraid. The fine old-fashioned story had, so far, gone as it should. But suppose, at the last minute, the son failed to meet the boat? Was he really the upstanding young man we all imagined? Did the story have some hidden catch?

Long after dark, we came to Callao. The boat moved silently toward the dimly lit dock. All of us were on the landward side, pressed close to the rail. Bonus Notches was very quiet. His wife's veil was once more tangling with her spectacles. "I don't see Tom," she said, and we all told her, with one voice, it was too soon on a night like this to see Tom.

The gangplank was lowered. Bonus Notches leaned far over the rail, his eyes searching the darkness. He raised his arm awkwardly, ready to wave. None of us seemed to breathe. All the faces on the dock were pale ovals, lifted toward us. Then suddenly, in the gloom, a voice called, "Dad! Mother!" And Bonus Notches answered, "Son!"

There was Tom. Even better than we imagined. Slender, straight, handsome. A strange sound, between tears and laughter, rose from all our throats. Tom strode up the gangplank, clasped his father and mother to his heart. Over and over, they said each other's names. They did not need any other words.

Bonus Notches did not forget his friends. He introduced each one of us to Tom. I do not remember anything we said. I only know we promised to keep in touch. Then we travelers from a dozen countries on two continents went our separate ways, into the darkness on the shore.

Notes and Index

Notes

1. Eric Sharp, "The 'Retirement in Florida' Dream Can Become a Nightmare for Some," *Detroit Free Press,* September 9, 1973.
2. Alexis de Tocqueville, *Democracy in America,* vol. II (New York: Vintage Books, 1955), p. 4.
3. Morton Puner, *To the Good Long Life* (New York: Universe Books, 1974), p. 13.
4. William H. Masters and Virginia E. Johnson, "The Human Sexual Response: The Aging Female and the Aging Male," in *Middle Age and Aging,* ed. B. L. Neugarten (Chicago: University of Chicago Press, 1968), p. 269.

Index

ABOUT THE EDITOR

Gerald Leinwand is Professor of Education and Dean of the School of Education at the Bernard M. Baruch College of the City University of New York. Dr. Leinwand received his B.A., M.S., and Ph.D. degrees from New York University, and he also holds an M.A. from Columbia University. He is the author of numerous magazine articles and four books: *The Pageant of World History; The Pageant of American History; The American Constitution: A Tutor-Text;* and a college text, *Teaching History and the Social Studies in Secondary Schools.*

ABOUT THE AUTHORS

Gordon E. Moss is an assistant professor of sociology at Eastern Michigan University. He received his Ph.D. in medical sociology from the State University of New York at Buffalo and holds a master's degree in sociology from Rutgers. He is the author of a book, *Illness, Immunity, and Social Interaction: The Dynamics of Biosocial Resonation,* and is active in research and publication in the area of social stress and disease. He is a member of the Southeastern Michigan Consortium on Gerontology and the Humanities, and he teaches a course on social gerontology.

Walter G. Moss is an associate professor of history at Eastern Michigan University. He received his Ph.D. from Georgetown University and his B.S. from Xavier University in Ohio. He has made various scholarly contributions in the field of history, and has acted since January 1973 as the project director of the Southeastern Michigan Consortium on Gerontology and the Humanities. He has been recognized as one of the Outstanding Educators of America for 1974-1975.